The Life And Time Of A Country Surgeon

The Good And The Bad

James W. Sampsel

authorHOUSE®

AuthorHouse™
1663 Liberty Drive
Bloomington, IN 47403
www.authorhouse.com
Phone: 1-800-839-8640

© 2011 James W. Sampsel. All rights reserved.

No part of this book may be reproduced, stored in a retrieval system, or transmitted by any means without the written permission of the author.

First published by AuthorHouse   7/26/2011

ISBN: 978-1-4634-0995-1 (sc)
ISBN: 978-1-4634-0994-4 (hc)
ISBN: 978-1-4634-0992-0 (e)

Library of Congress Control Number: 2011909131

Printed in the United States of America

Any people depicted in stock imagery provided by Thinkstock are models, and such images are being used for illustrative purposes only.
Certain stock imagery © Thinkstock.

This book is printed on acid-free paper.

Because of the dynamic nature of the Internet, any web addresses or links contained in this book may have changed since publication and may no longer be valid. The views expressed in this work are solely those of the author and do not necessarily reflect the views of the publisher, and the publisher hereby disclaims any responsibility for them.

Acknowledgements:

To Becky Hilbert, former head of Medical Records of Memorial Hospital, for typing and editing. To June Ray for being a great secretary and typist. Diana Salyers, one of our nurses, for producing a list of nurses that worked at Memorial during our time. My wife, Dolly, reviewing, always encouraging, for putting up with me during the writing, and most important, for creating a family background that supported country surgery.

Dedication

This book is dedicated to our deceased daughter, Mary. She was an avowed liberal among conservatives. She never knew what I did while away from home so much!

Contents

Introduction:	xi
Preliminary Happenings Childhood And Beyond:	1
Surgery Training:	9
The Military:	22
How We Came To Country Surgery:	31
Memorial Hospital Of Union County	33
Legal Entanglements	57
The American Board Of Surgery And The American College Of Surgeons	61
Nurses	65
My Uncle Charlie, Other Doctors And Events Of Influence!	72
Case Reports With Human Interest:	85
Innovations And Inventions During Our Time:	98
The Scope Of Surgical Problems In Productive Years:	104
Research, Surgical And Other:	138
Finis:	157

Introduction:

Friends and workers come by, around home, see my writing, and ask: "What is your book about?" I tell them "it's about the early days of our hospital" to express a topic that might catch their interest, without going into detail. I know they are thinking: why is this old codger writing a book? Actually, reasons for writing books are endless, but they center around recording accomplishments, perhaps some visionary scheme describing some complex current situation, political or religious, science, history, all about given times and places. The ego of the writer is a feature; he envisions his ideas to be of some general interest.

This book is no exception; it's about ordinary people and life's events, hopefully of interest, related to a forty-five year practice of country surgery, during a certain time, in a small central Ohio town. Many aspects of the human condition are covered by depictions of incidents leading up to and including productive years. An attempt is made to combine the concepts of random events that shape every life, with the addition of planned, envisioned, devised activities. The latter, not too often thought of as acquired, unique functions of the evolved human brain. These exploits all mixed in to account a time when the practice of general surgery encompassed multiple specialties, for good or for bad.

My youngest son saw the title that included the "good and the bad". He laughed and said: "including the bad would create lots more interest". But it does not take scientific observation to know, that about everything and everybody contain good and bad phases, aspects, characteristics, depending on impressions, opinions, from "Where you stand". Time has to be added to the equation – consider cigarettes, food, guns, fire, rain, even Irish Whiskey, "a little bit is good, too much will kill you!"

There are certain impressions that come to the elder mind, guiding the major components of this book, not occurring in the young. Young folks tend to live from day to day, few perhaps planning, fortunately not being able to predict or see the future. The same obtained for the author in formative years and in productive times, too busy with daily tasks to record events or to give proper evaluation to relationships. But, as one gets old, losing physical abilities, looking back often; the mind transcends time, and random events become prominent features. The first for each individual being where and when you were born. Were you breast fed, in a loving family? Influence of contemporaries, when young and impressionable, time and world affairs, all add to the formation.

A country surgeon has all these environmental influences on his production, along with the inner genetic elements he's been dealt. Hopefully, they all mesh together giving him a privilege to operate on people, master established technique and delve into the cognitive aspects. Along with the science, one is not to forget an essential quest for understanding and appreciating various personalities along the way.

Preliminary Happenings Childhood And Beyond:

Modern child psychologists should have a field day trying to decipher how events from first perceptive years can influence later life. Self-impressions of my childhood, many good, are dominated by the bads. For instance, there was a juvenile episode where I stuck my fist through a pane-glass window in a deserted house, on a dare from Peter Aponick, a young Greek accomplice. Or, tearing up a note to my parents, carried by my sister, from my third grade teacher, telling them what a bad boy I was in class. Miss Garrity, the third grade teacher, left the room, a pack of "life savers" on her desk; I confiscated the candy and distributed it to kids in the front row. Guess what I got from Miss Garrity?

But a more serious charge that never became known, was when I inadvertently started a small forest fire. The rationalization for this move was complex: We lived on a mountaintop, Shenandoah Heights; forest fires were frequent, and I had been with my Dad to a few, volunteering to help control them. So, one day I came by some matches and decided to start small fires in the woods and practice putting them out, you know what's coming: one got away and I scrammed home. Fortunately, men from the Fire Department came and put out the fire before a lot of damage occurred. No one ever knew that I started it, but I spent weeks worrying every time a police car came by our street.

The bads continued for me into 5th, 6th and 7th grades. I just never got the picture for academics. One time in 6th grade, I submitted a paper to the teacher, Miss Tabor, a friend of my Aunt Sissie, teacher of English in another school. My submitted paper was so bad that Miss Tabor insisted I take it home, show it to my father, requesting him to sign it so she would know I showed it to him. At the showing he was reading a book, and he used the book to beat my behind up the stairs to my room. He said it was so bad, that he refused to sign it. I had a hard time explaining this to Miss Tabor, but she believed me.

In 7th grade we had Miss Barrett, a "stickler for detail" about arithmetic problems involving proportions, decimals and fractions. I had my hands slapped daily with Miss Barrett's ruler. One day, Mr. Murray, the regional school supervisor, an uncle of my friend Frank Sullivan, asked Miss Barrett how come his nephew was not doing well in her class? She said: "Stand up James Sampsel. There is the reason". We never thought of bringing information like that home, fearing further punishment.

There were all kinds of other bad incidents, fights, chases, near accidents, some profound, others minor. But examining them all in retrospect, I find the situation strangely paradoxical because, I was the first born into a loving home. We lived in a row house with a small entryway, and a fifty-foot square back yard. Our family was poor, about the same as everyone on the street, living from day-to-day, most working directly or indirectly associated with the coal mines.

My Dad had multiple jobs starting as a lineman for the P.P. and L. (The Pennsylvania Power and Light); also he arranged music for local dance bands. He was a pianist and composed numerous popular songs and etudes. Notedly, along with his daily striving to make us a living, he was a strict disciplinarian, fair and sometimes understanding. Subtracting from the bads were the times he took us for walks in the woods, which were just down and across the street from our house. Or the many fishing trips for trout, piano lessons that we objected to, and his introducing us to classical music, were all a definite good!

My mother was Irish, Marguerite Brennan, a beautiful woman, subjective, always a housewife and mother, always worried about my dad when he was out working during thunder storms. She hardly ever left the house, perhaps rarely for rides in the country or for family picnics. Her primary tasks were having babies, keeping us all fed and happy with mild discipline. But one time I remember she broke a window when she threw a shoe at my brother, Bill, for some infraction, and it missed.

Family get-togethers with relatives were frequent and looked forward to. Christmas with tree and presents, the 4th of July with fireworks were the primary events – somehow I developed a leaning toward the "downtown" house of my paternal grandmother and her daughter, my maiden Aunt

"Sissie", going there on weekends, some holidays and summer vacations. Surely, the individual attention I got there was a prominent factor in this move. It's where I became a loved "fat little boy", eating up a storm on weekends, because my grandmother made great meals for her "boarders", a common practice in those days, to have boarders come to the house twice a day for their meals.

To confuse the childhood picture more, at the visits to my grandmother's house, my memories are of pursuing a double life: on the one hand, for the good, I made model airplanes, also became infatuated with a toy microscope set that someone gave me at Christmas. There were prepared slides of insects, bacteria, and I looked at blood cells and creatures in pond water.

On the other hand, as the bad part of the double life: I remember being part of a kids gang, hanging out at a near-by railroad yard, using foul language, playing war with wooden guns and rubber band bullets, even getting chased by cops when we stole broken watermelons from box cars with open doors, and running off into the hills. I guess being a nice boy on Sundays, gong to church with grandma, even singing in the choir that my Aunt Sissie directed, overcame the bad and set me on the righter course.

Somewhat later, perhaps at the 8th or 9th grade levels, an event creating a lot of emotional effort, never at the time connecting with enthusiasm toward my path as a physician, occurred in a sandlot football game. I was running with the ball, and a fat kid, Fuzzy McGraw tackled me, and somehow I ran into his outstretched arm, fracturing the radius and ulna, resulting in a bizarre angle below the elbow. We hurriedly took him to the local Locust Mountain State Hospital and my uncle Charlie was on duty as an extern in the Emergency Room. They invited me in to watch the reduction and cast. I can still smell the drop ether anesthetic. The same ether smell permeated the whole hospital and I came to like it. By the way, when we took Fuzzy McGraw home, arm in a cast, his mother "threw a fit", she reacted with anguish and hints of punishment, not for the poor boy's infirmity, but for some unknown sense of misconduct on our part, resulting in this unwanted expense.

But this was my first venture into the halls of a hospital that resulted in years of inspiring thoughts about becoming a physician. Next, with the permissions of the surgeons, Charlie took me to watch an operation. I remember putting on hospital garb, with cap and uncomfortable mask, in the doctor's dressing room, and Charlie told me not to touch anything when we entered the operating room. It was all bright lights, strange smells, and vague exposed organs – and I had a sense of relief, viewing the moon and stars on a clear night as I left the hospital and scrambled up the mountain, home.

Despite the scary initiation, I was drawn to watching other procedures. I would run down the mountain, run up the back stairs to the dressing room, gear up and watch operations whenever Charlie would call. Eventually, Dr. Leach, the Chief Surgeon, had the nurses teach me how to scrub and I began to hold retractors at these operations. I remember having mixed feelings there, at first of being bothersome, especially when Charlie returned to school, but Dr. Leach and Dr. Brudzinski, the Assistant Surgeon, both seemed genuinely glad to see me each time I showed up. Early on, I was embarrassed to accept their invitations to lunch in the hospital dining room, but eventually I got to know everyone, nurses, aides, and people in the clinics. There were lots of other great things happened for me at Locust Mountain State Hospital, and I returned many times during vacations from school, always with productive greeting from folks there.

More Random Events Contributing To Country Surgery:

A cascade of happenings in everyone's life shapes one's future, frequently, without personal effort or input, perhaps just being at a certain time and place, like random events described in a book, "The Drunkard's Walk" by Leonard Mlodinow. I "zig-zagged" through significant chance episodes, starting from a position of naïve teen aging, working, playing ball, hoping to get to college, but thinking about working instead, being OK. Then, Uncle Charlie called and said: "Get your application to the pre-med class at Penn State". I sent it in but a letter came and informed me: "The class is filled." One day after we received that letter, my dad took me by the hand, we careened to the office of our State Representative, Dr. Iver D. Fenton, in Mahonoy City, Pa., and I still have visuals of his office with stained glass windows and doors. My dad told him: "My son wants to be a doctor, and we got this letter from the State College turning him down". The doctor said: "We'll see what we can do". Two weeks later, we got another letter from the Admissions Dean, welcoming me to the School of Chemistry and Physics in pre-med. I guess you must say that random connections started me on the academic path.

The School of Chemistry and Physics at Penn State in 1939, had about ten pre-med students, mixed with engineers, physics and chemistry majors; science courses were accented. My tuition for the first quarter was $40.00, in addition, a refundable $10.00 to cover laboratory breakage. Room rent was $3.00-$5.00 per month and a good meal at Fred's Restaurant was $.50. I managed to get on the freshman and varsity baseball teams as a catcher, resulting in a few training tables and a job at the SPS House for my meals. My room was at Mrs.Kramer's house, around the corner from College Avenue, at 127 N. Atherton Street. She rented two rooms to students; one pre-med student just moved out that had an acceptance to John's Hopkins in Baltimore, a place we all held in reverence.

Learning How To Study:

A significant event for me was when Herman Panzer, another pre-med student, moved from the Jewish Fraternity to the empty room across the hall from me, at Mrs. Kramer's. Herman was a top-notch student, who had difficulty studying with the noise and partying in the chaotic fraternity house. Lucky for me, he decided to move to our quiet rooming house on North Atherton Street. We became friends, and I gradually acquired his study habits, writing down and memorizing complex organic chemistry conversions, math equations, physics problems – we developed a routine of studying hard for three-four hours, then ambling down to watch the girls go by at the corner room. I got passable grades before Herman arrived, but I learned from him the skill of intense studying. He was the number one student in the Organic Chemistry course, and I was close to the top, at number two. This turned out to have momentous importance because Dr. Olwein, the organic chemistry professor, was also the pre-med advisor, and would you believe, also a baseball fan. He surprised me on an interview when he asked me where I wanted to go to medical school? I nervously responded with my selections, previously suggested by my uncle Charlie: Western Reserve University in Cleveland and the University of Pennsylvania in Philadelphia.

Mailing A Letter Determines Future Course:

How random events influence your way, only when you look back on activities, never more than simply dropping a letter into a mailbox: probably from recommendation of Dr.Olwein at Penn State, I received an acceptance to the medical school at Western Reserve. With this in mind, visiting medical schools in Philadelphia on a class trip, I consulted Uncle Charlie in Bristol, Pa, a suburb where he was practicing. He gave me a $100.00 check to put in the envelope with my acceptance letter. His advice was for me to quickly mail it if they did not guarantee my admission at the University of Pennsylvania – They did not, so I immediately dropped it in a mailbox. One day later, after a Greyhound bus trip back to State College, I had a telegram on the bed at Mrs. Kramer's. It informed me of a positive admission from their committee. I informed them of a refusal and looked to Cleveland with eagerness.

The medical school at Western Reserve full-filled all my expectations – it was housed in one huge building, multiple stories high, blocks long and wide. Walking in front of it, I looked up and thought: "How lucky I am to be here." Close by, just across the mall, were University Hospitals, down the street, the Allen Memorial Medical Library, Severance Hall, home of the Cleveland Orchestra, the Art Museum, and Hessler Road just around the corner; where Dick Watts, arranged for my quarters in Mrs. Sullivan's home. Richard Ward Watts was from a prominent Cleveland family. He and I were the first two pre-meds taken from Penn State to Western Reserve. Richard and our friend, Jim Shumaker acquired quarters across the street from Mrs. Sullivan's on Hessler Road at Grandma's unique house, where they occupied the third floor. Grandma's daughter Amy Good was married to a physician, Dr. Good, a pediatrician that gave us lots of counsel through the years. Hessler Road was an unequaled street in the City of Cleveland, a dead end, with a life of its own, individual houses separated by small entryways, wide old sidewalks, and small gardens in front. The narrow street itself, allegedly the only one in the city paved with bricks made of wood. It was a block removed from busy Euclid Avenue. University people lived there, mostly all students or teachers. There was hardly anyway you could avoid ardent studying if you lived on this street.

Dick Watts became a cardiologist and a major contributor to Western Reserve Medical School. Jim Shumaker practiced internal medicine on the West Coast, and gave half a million dollars to Ashland College for a new science building.

The curriculum at Western Reserve Medical School, for the class of 1946, speeded up because of the war, was all anatomy with human dissection every morning for about six months. Afternoons, microscopic histology, hematology, embryology, occupied your time. Months went by and we embarked into neurology with an impressive Dr. Scharrer, and with a renowned Dr. Carl Wiggers, into physiology, the study of functional motion, especially the cardiovascular system. The Science of Genetics then was limited to Gregor Mendel's black and white peas. Pathology was made enlightening by Howard T. Karsner, another of the world's most prestigious textbook authors, bringing together all the previous disciplines. Pharmacology, taught by the ancient Dr. Sollman, author of the thickest textbook known to man, and in whose class smart-ass guys threw paper airplanes around the back of the room during lectures, was one of the least disciplined courses.

The clinical aspects of our education came on rapidly, mostly in the clinics and wards across the mall, of University Hospitals where we spent time with doctors of Internal Medicine, Surgery, Obstetrics and Gynecology, Pediatrics and Psychiatry, the latter along with seeing contagious diseases at City Hospital, a 5,000 bed city facility on the other side of town. We were also observers at a Cleveland Veteran's Hospital where German prisoners of war served as ward aides and service people. The City Hospital housed a collection of psychotic patients, and our only exposure to these individuals was a great course taught by one Dr. Louie Karnash. We were entertained at City Hospital with observations of diseases no longer prevalent: syphilitic brain dementia, Korsakoff's Syndrome, thoracoplasties for tuberculous lung cavities, and cases of active or delayed deformities from polio myelitis. These serious conditions were reduced by antibiotics and vaccines, but learning about methods for diagnosis and therapy were crucial for a physician's education.

The fields of Gynecology and Obstetrics were taught at McDonald House, part of University Hospitals. The Pap smear for diagnosing cervical cancer was coming into being, and we were studying the shed surface cells to identify stages of this common and devastating malady – it was all the rage, new and exciting.

Our introduction to obstetrics also exciting, was by way of home delivery. The University was always in touch with the minority community, and pregnancy clinics were always busy. When patients went into labor at home, they would somehow get access to a telephone, call the hospital, and two of us; senior students would be dispatched in a hospital car, always with difficulty finding the address. Into back alleys and up old stairs, we would arrive with our bags to assay the situation, examine for cervical dilatations, and call back to the hospital for a Resident to be present during the delivery. The Resident had to be on the scene for us to get credit for the procedure, and we had to have a certain number of deliveries to pass the course. We got to be pretty good at judging the time for the baby to appear, and we were usually surprised at the cooperation plus the acclimation of the older folks around, during and after each event. Sometimes we even helped to name the new arrival. The telephone rang several times a day in the waiting room where we waited our turn, while mostly studying and listening to classical music on records, part of the enjoyable experience with this senior discipline that sticks in my mind. It was followed by graduation and the struggle to get the ideal internship.

Surgery Training:

Everyone had to show up for the Saturday morning conferences, starting at nine o'clock, no matter what service you were on. It was really a mortality and morbidity meeting where everyone's decisions were challenged by the chief and usually several other visitants. I was "scared to death" there with the fear of being called on as an intern, but after starting my speech course, I would volunteer opinions, good or bad, and I really think this helped my chances to continue in the residency; for it was a competitive program. Although we all had respect for each other, we were all competing each year for next year's job. We started with fifteen surgical interns and everyone knew that there would be only four left after four or five years of training. A few dropped out for various reasons, financial, the military, romances, and a few went into specialties like orthopedics, genitourinary or NET. But most all had to go on military duty after two years, and most had their job, at a given level, guaranteed on return.

Why would we compete for a job that had a starting pay at zero dollars per month, but you got board, room, and laundry? There was every other night off, and we worked every other weekend. On the weekends off, we often spent time in the library and many nights off we just stayed with some critical patient. Not to make us martyrs or anything, but it was just everyone's expected routine, somewhat akin to a hermit priest in some far off abbey, no chance for disturbing outside influences, beside eating and sleeping; all activity was devoted to the tasks at hand.

And the initial interview to get the job was interesting: you made a written application, but you were called in front of four or five surgeons, including the Chief Dr. Lenhart, in my time, and there were all kinds of probing questions to this recently graduated med student: How were your finances? Why did you choose surgery? How about your love life? In my case there was a plus when I told them my wife was working. But a few of the other candidates were from wealthy families, and had no financial difficulties. This was fortunate for them; because our pay scale went from zero the first year, fifty dollars per month the second year, seventy five the third, one hundred the fourth, and one fifty if you stayed for five. So, I guess the big advantage of striving for this position was the association with the University and the chance that you could end up with some sort of an academic appointment. The big argument among us, at the time, centered about not the money, but the possibility of learning more clinical surgery at an increased pace in some large private hospital. However, the chance of getting back into any academic setting would be practically zero without university type training and for me at that time, it appeared to be the best course.

The course included private surgical services, the so-called free wards where the Chief Residents did most of the operating, and all of these combined with emergency room call. Dr. Beck's service for three months combined neuro-surgery with cardiac procedures, the latter in its infancy. There were also rotations through orthopedics, genitourinary, and NET. Obligations varied between three months to six months on these sessions with more time and emphasis on the general surgery, pathology, and research. There was considerable overlap of services depending on changes related to external and internal random factors, like for one, the institution of medical and surgical insurance developed, markedly reducing the census within the free wards, and likewise the number of cases for the resident staff. The University, in order to preserve the integrity of residency training, encompassed the surgical problems of the Cleveland State Mental Hospital. A review of my experiences with some of these provisions at various times, the events, the personalities, associated with each one and their influence on a country surgeon are here recorded:

Private surgery at Hanna House, the original Lakeside Hospital:

Hanna House was one large section of University Hospitals, in a separate building, devoted to private patients. There were about ten surgeons of various specialties on the staff there, all with University appointments, supervising interns and residents, who ran the floors of private and semiprivate rooms. There was always a first year intern with a second and sometimes a third year resident in attendance. You wrote orders at the nurses station, and visited the patients frequently, especially when the visiting surgeon arrived and you went on "rounds" to get the direction and opinions of the visitants. It was here you learned how to write orders on the chart in a systematic and efficient manner. Actually, the nurses often pointed out what was important for patient needs: diet and pain medications were paramount, then directions for pulse rates, respiration rates, body temperatures and blood pressure data at certain time intervals, no monitor with automatic recordings then, all needed to be recorded on the chart by nurses so that one could assay the patient's progress at a glance, good or bad. Also, the resident or intern made a note about some incident of significance almost daily. It behooved you to appear on the floors daily at about 6:00 A.M. to evaluate the sick patients before going to surgery, which was always at eight o'clock, and the visitant you were assisting would always ask about this or that patient, how they did through the night, and hopefully you had seen the sick ones, reviewed their chart, and be able to report on it. Actually, this activity was a chore, but was made easier by the intense concern you would develop for each individual, as if he or she were your own patient, and you would try to keep pain and apprehension at a minimum when attending to the various floor procedures. For there were many like: starting IV's, passing gastric tubes for suction, supervising chest suction, changing wound dressings and drainage tubes, blood transfusions, and many more. The opportunity to see the patient initially on admission, get the history and do the examination was a way to be introduced to a wide variety of surgical problems.

All this was mixed with the usual morning surgery, helping as first or second assistant, rarely getting to do part of the operations, often eagerly doing closures. The operating room schedule was made up each day by Miss Angel or Miss Barry, the boss nurses, posted each night before, and you had to get the elevator to the eighth floor to see where and when you were on. Many times your scheduled activity was interrupted by emergencies, trauma, or unforeseen complications on the floor, leaving the operating surgeon with no assistant, and rarely you were happy to be late, depending on how you judged the individual doctor.

All the surgeons on the private service had different personalities, some volunteered on the free ward services. Toddy Sloane was old, feeble, had Parkinson's disease, should have retired, but somehow operated with our help. Frank Gibson, one of the older visitants, the doctor's doctor, anatomist, had big strong hands, perfect technique, knowledgeable, a joy to work with. I remember one instance where we had a patient come in one night with intestinal obstruction, x-ray showed the typical ladder pattern, but I saw a large gallstone shadow in the mid abdomen. When I called him about the case, I mentioned gallstone ileus, a somewhat unusual condition where a large gallstone erodes through the gallbladder wall, and believe it or not, continues to erode into the intestinal tract, gets into the terminal ileum where the bowel caliber is reduced, sticks there and obstructs the small bowel. Dr. Gibson came in, we operated about midnight, and the patient did well. The doctor made a special effort, after showing the huge gallstone to the family, to give it to me as a symbol for my making the diagnosis.

Other cases that stick in my memory were those with Dr. Daryl Shaw, a plastic surgeon that was always at odds with the nursing staff and also was never a favorite of Dr. Holden, the chief. But Dr. Shaw was a brilliant guy and we all knew it. He had great research ideas and taught all kinds of plastic surgical principles, like incisions along skin lines, tendon repairs, and skin grafts with the Paget dermatome. Dr. Shaw got himself very unpopular by constantly complaining to Miss Angel that the nurse she would send in to assist was inadequate. He led a troubled life but he was always nice to the residents, gave me a plastic needle holder when I left his service that I treasured.

There were several physicians on the private service that came over from City Hospital, and we were always eager to help them in the O.R. One was Mittie Lambright, a thoracic specialist, mostly did lung resections and his technique was flawless. He was the only Negro doctor on the staff at University, a big, strong athletic type, made me think about going to City Hospital for an extra year in thoracic surgery. The other surgeon from City Hospital that taught us everything about thyroid surgery was Brown Dobbins. His ideas about removing the entire gland for toxicosis and tumor were in the forefront of the field. His emphasis was careful identification and preservation of the laryngeal nerves and parathyroid glands. Many times when I did my own thyroid operations, I thought about his contributions. Identification and preserving small vessels to the parathyroids was a task that you always worried about.

Eldon Weckesser, another general surgeon, an associate professor, probably lost out for the professorship because of his time in the South Pacific with the Lakeside Unit, like many of our chief residents and visitants. Weck was a gentle guy, always optimistic, caring, cautious, questioning, had a big private surgical practice. He always had a lot of respect for the residents and the University.

The most flamboyant and efficient general surgeon in the group was Frank Barry. Frank was an associate professor, and under Carl Lenhart, the old chief, he was "top dog". He did everything: gallbladders, skin to skin in 15-20 minutes, pinned fractured hips, I helped him do babies with pyloric stenosis. We did pyloric myotomies once in a set of twins for this condition. We published one of the rare cases of spurious aneurysm of the hepatic artery together. He was the guy that told me: "Your job as resident will always be here when you return from the military". However, when I returned after three years away, Frank was still on staff, but his status had been reduced by Bill Holden, the new chief, appointed after Carl Lenhart retired. Actually I did get my job back when I returned and I had three years under Dr. Holden being the department chief.

Dr. Holden was a different type of surgeon, pipe smoking, Ivy League trained, research oriented, not often a happy type, married into a prominent Cleveland family, had great Saturday morning meetings where we all had to defend our decisions. It was where I first heard the term "through the retro-spectroscope things can frequently look different", the words of John Kralick, one of the residents a year my junior, who ultimately became chief of cardiac surgery at a large Cleveland Hospital. I have used this phrase a lot in my career since then. For me there was a bad Saturday morning when I had to report a case of an obese elderly man with right upper quadrant pain, admitted him one night, gave him fluids, pain meds and ordered x-rays for the morning. He went into shock, died suddenly in the morning. When I came to see him, they were wheeling him to the morgue. The autopsy showed that he had a ruptured gallbladder with generalized peritonitis. I had a difficult time explaining why I had not advised operation at midnight, perhaps he would have died anyway, but in the conference, I could only say that I would not let that happen again. There was probably something in his story or his physical exam that should have alerted me. By delving into individual cases like this in open discussions, most every surgical problem, technique, metabolism, operative indications, mistakes in judgement, reviewing x-rays and lab reports, was examined in detail, from the free and private services.

Multiple skills were acquired on the private services, but the primary learning experiences came on the so-called "free wards" at the University, two floors devoted to general surgery, one male and one female. They were the complete responsibility of the chief resident and his staff of underlings. When I was an intern, all the chief residents had returned from the military and service in World War II. They were all experienced surgeons, Jake Wells, John Bond, John Cooper and Frank Portman. All went into country surgical practices, Wells and Portman in Ohio, others in remote states.

I had three chief residents in general surgery ahead of me by a year or two, Byers Shaw, Tom Hancock and Jay Ankeney. They all had unique personalities, Byers was confident, moved right into any operation and I was always impressed with his surgical skills. Tom was a little more reserved, cautious, slower, quizzical, but competent. Byers and Tom became country surgeons in nearby Washington Courthouse, Jay Ankeney became chief of Cardiac Surgery at University Hospitals after a stint helping with the invention and perfection of the heart-lung machine at Jefferson Hospitals in Philadelphia, Pa. Jay and I spent many an evening and night, walking the halls, going to the emergency room, making rounds. He would say: "Sammy you're wrong" about this or that diagnosis, and if I was ever proven right, he would never acknowledge it, as happened several times. One of these episodes transpired in the emergency room when we were both wrong when an obese middle aged lady came in with abdominal pain, some tenderness, normal menstrual history, and we missed a pregnancy caught on abdominal x-ray. We couldn't believe it when we saw the films. She delivered a seven-month fetus the next day. But the emergency room was always full of surprises. I remember my phone ringing at night, the long walk from my dormitory room, into the tunnel, past the basement pool table room, onto a squeaky elevator, to the emergency room or a floor problem. Walking the dark halls of a hospital at night has always had a strange appeal for me, and at University I was always thinking how lucky I was to have the run of this great place.

The residents above you on the charity wards would often let you do part of an operation under their guidance. I remember the first operation I did from start to finish was a saphenous vein dissection and multiple peripheral ligations. I went to my room that night happy, and thinking that I had arrived. It was in this state of mind I did a lot of practice knot tying with suture, hemostat handling, learning to open and close hemostats by simply twisting with thumb and fingers, and needle holder manipulations.

Pediatric Surgery Service:

The pediatric service at University was housed in a big separate building, called Babies and Childrens Hospital. It had a mixture of private and charity cases, with a variety of staff surgeons and residents operating. There was no pediatric surgical specialty per se then, but one of my class mates, Bob Izant, after his training in general surgery and a stint in the Navy, went to Boston, studied with Drs. Ladd and Gross there, eventually returning to be the chief of Babies and Childrens for twenty years or so. During our time of training, the pediatric surgery was handled by several different physicians, but the most prominent was Edward Gerrish. Eddie was a general surgeon, eminent in Dr. Holden's realm, short, funny, but he could be sarcastic, believed negative criticism was the best method to enhance training of surgeons. I have one episode with him etched on my brain when late one morning, into an afternoon, while I was holding a retractor in a case of some poor infant with esophageal atresia. We were struggling to uncover both ends of the stenosis, and I fell forward, nearly falling asleep in view of the slow dissection. Dr. Gerrish said: "Sammy, get your sleep elsewhere, damn it, you sleep too much and you eat too much". I thought my "goose was cooked" for the next year's appointment, but I guess he was overruled by other members of the review board. Dr. Gerrish later became an executive vice president in the American College of Surgeons, in Chicago, dealing with yearly meetings.

Immeasurable experiences were garnered at Babies and Childrens Hospital on our service there, three months inclusive, a year on and off. Pediatrics was just becoming a specialty then, and we had exposure to the many tragic and impossible problems like bile duct atresias, extensive tracheoesophageal disconnections, bowel and anal atresias, Hirschsprung's disease of the colon, some operable, many not. We did a lot of plastic repairs of cleft lip defects, and handled a lot of burns in children. Finding scalp veins and other venous access for fluid therapy in kids was always damnable. Pyloric stenosis was a common problem cured by myotomy at the pyloric sphincter. Very few of these problems did we see or treat at Memorial, but a common condition was inguinal hernia in the newborn, and our experience with this condition in training paid off immensely in practice later on. I acquired confidence in making the incision near the transverse skin fold, isolate the sac and ligate it, be aware of the non descended testicle, that had to be handled in one way or another. These were delicate tissues and the key word was <u>careful.</u>

Dr. Beck's Service:

"We can start now, Dr. Simple has arrived". This was a frequent morning,

8:00 A.M. greeting from Claude Beck as I would come into the O.R., and we would turn down a scalp flap to remove some poor fellow's brain tumor, or fracture a stenotic mitral valve. One of my three-month services was with Claude Beck, M.D. one of two remaining living and working trainees of William H. Halstead, of John's Hopkins fame, the father of our American style of surgery training. Now for me, a lowly surgical intern, able to sit in Dr. Beck's office, hear him discuss cases with Dr. Fred Coller of Michigan, the other only living Halstead trainee, was like going to heaven. Dr. Beck was older, a big man, slightly bent over, obese, red nosed with a whiney voice, a W.C. Fields, the comedian, look alike. He was a legend in his own time at the University, always at odds with the department chairman, Dr. Holden, and an enigma for the medical cardiologists because of his innovative cardiac procedures. Every day was an exciting time for us on this service, from clinical surgery in the morning, where we were fracturing mitral valves or excising brain tumors, to the dog lab in the afternoon where we were ligating coronary arteries, producing heart ischemia, then reversing the circulation by anastomosing grafts from the aorta to the coronary sinus. We actually did a few patients with this concept after it proved successful in the dogs, and it had modest success. Another innovative maneuver of Dr. Beck's for cardiac ischemia was to put asbestos into the pericardial sac, causing inflammation, and hopefully bringing a blood supply to the myocardium. These, and his repeated efforts to improve patients with mitral stenosis by fracturing valves, made the medical cardiologists, led by Dr. Harold Feil, to think of him as a charlatan.

I remember several weekly hospital conferences, when various departments would present their work: Envision this scene, an amphitheater filled with residents, interns, visiting doctors, Dr. Beck would get up before our presentation, place a recording device up front, and ask anyone with objections or criticisms to give their name before expressing their ideas. It was an effort to quell the underlying objections to a sizeable mortality rate in these high-risk patients. Dr. Harold Feil, the Chief of Medical Cardiology, had a son-in-law, Herm Hellerstein, a great fellow, would brag about his ability to read ECG's so thoroughly that "he could tell the color of the elevator boy's cap" by the shape of his electrocardiogram. Dr. Hellerstein was a very sharp guy that was at the forefront of developing the ECG, the electrocardiogram, - when it came about from the Einthoven Triangle, that we had in the hall, outside the operating room, hooked up to Dr. Beck's patients as we operated on them. We couldn't put the

ECG in the O.R. for fear of sparks causing explosions when mixed with anesthetic vapors.

A distinct positive innovation sponsored by Dr. Beck and his chief resident, David Leighniger, despite mild criticism by medical cardiologists, was the introduction of cardiac resuscitation to the Cleveland area and beyond. The concepts of shocking the heart that was in ventricular fibrillation, or standstill on ECG, along with open chest massage of the failing heart, were all maneuvers that we actually used. I can remember my awe, as I had my first encounter, directly massaging a failing heart in Dr. Beck's operating room. I guess you could call it courage to slash open the chest, spread ribs, insert your gloved hand to massage the heart directly. Several patients actually survived these measures, but many did not. Notoriety for the concept of cardiac resuscitation was furthered when Dr. Beck published several papers on the subject and his catch words were that he was saving "The hearts too young to die". And always, he brought up the story of unconscious patients at John's Hopkins being resuscitated by the Fire Department with their pulmotor breathing machines, and he thought this should be a medical doctor responsibility. There were several local physicians, not part of the University, that championed Dr. Beck's causes, one Dr. Hossler, a surgeon, and another Dr. Titche, a general practitioner. They always came to the conferences, sat in the front rows, and I can hear Dr. Beck calling on Dr. Titche, "Dr. Titche, tell us about your patient's satisfaction with our operation".

Dr. Dave Leighniger was a faithful chief resident for Dr. Beck, all the years I was at University. He ran the dog lab, assisted and did a lot of the surgery, neuro, cardiac, and other less dramatic. He was mild mannered, a workhorse, did everything, day and night. I never saw him angry. I learned a lot from him about anastomosing small vessels in the dog heart. We had Brendyl Bull dogs for cardiac research because their hearts were large, but their vessels were still small. The sad part of Dave's tenure as Dr. Beck's resident was that he had the impression that four years there would qualify him to take the exams of the American Board of Surgery, but they changed the policy and he had to get two more years training in general surgery. So for us, spending three months with a former Halstead resident was a distinct honor, for David, the four-year honor was not enough.

What did I take from my time on Dr. Beck's service? I guess you could say there was the ego bolstering subconscious feeling of being a part of innovative heart surgery and resuscitation. We did use the latter skills frequently in different forms, with country surgery. I learned not to panic in the presence of massive blood loss, and that sometimes-terrible situations have to be created to accomplish the good. Drilling holes in the cranium and taking down skull flaps we rarely had to do in the country, but it was good to be exposed.

The experience with small blood vessel anastomosis came in handy many times.

Other Services:
The G.U. Service:

On the genitourinary service our primary operation was TUR, transurethral resection of obstructing prostatic enlargement. It was an entirely boring procedure for an assistant. All you did was standby and use the evacuator to remove prostatic chips as the operator did all the cutting through the cystoscope. Each one of those operations was an eternity, and as an assistant you wearily looked out the 8th floor window, onto Lake Erie, sailboats flowing about, wishing you were there, before Dr. Williams or Dr. Jimmie Joelson would let you look into the cystoscope and perhaps manipulate the electronic cutting instrument once or twice. However, you tolerated that boredom for the opportunity the service gave you for assisting with nephrectomies in patients with kidney cancer or pyelonephritis, handling stone disease of the kidney, or more practical ureteral manipulation for same, and learning the intricacies of bladder repair after injury or disease. The other invaluable experience there was dealing with the Foley catheter and all the elaborate tricks necessary to get catheters by the obstructed urethra into the bladder. We saw a number of horrendous perineum infections secondary to obstructed and disrupted urethras, probably of gonococcal origin, perhaps related to the time and place; because we rarely saw the like at Memorial. Visualizing and interpreting intravenous pyelograms (IVP's) was high on the teaching list of the G.U. Service. This test with its intravenous dye injection, its visualization of the entire anatomical urinary system in detail, along with its demonstration of kidney function, became essential for a country surgeon when no other specialists were around. I don't remember seeing a lot of prostate cancer, and I don't know why? We never did radical operations for it, but there was also no known blood test like PSA, prostatic associated antigen. The stint on the G.U. service was made genial by the chief resident George Woodfin, a Texan, loved race horses, and he would have us all out his house for the Kentucky Derby, of course serving mint juleps.

The Orthopedic Service:
The orthopedic service was also made enjoyable by the personality of its chief resident, Mike Pardee. He was a quiet type guy, but a great teacher about plaster technique, and the valued experiences were centered about pinning hip fractures, plates and screws for tibia and arm fracture, as well as overhead traction devices for certain femur breaks. The boss on the orthopedic service was Dr. Herndon, an academic type that did extensive hip pinnings, made a big deal about it; he was slow but careful.

The Net Service:
Our NET service was spent primarily with Val Jordan, the chief, recently returned from the South Pacific, where he was stationed for some four or five years with the Lakeside Unit. Val was just a regular type guy, despite the fact that he was married to the sister of Bill Holden's wife. The vital thing we acquired on this service was the indications and technique to do tracheostomy for laryngeal obstruction, a common situation with children at that time, there being no IV steroids, no endotracheal tubes and only steam in a croup tent along with antibiotics. It was here that we learned about tracheostomy: "When in doubt do it".

Surgery At The Mental Institution:
After I and four or five other doctors returned from the military we were called into Dr. Holden's office for an explanation about the reduced number of patients on the free wards, and that we were acquiring the surgical services at the Cleveland State Mental Hospital. This was a giant mental institution with five thousand patients, quartered into various buildings and wards, spread around a huge campus. I don't know how Western Reserve and University Hospitals made the arrangements, but we had this three or six month service out there doing the surgery and examining the populace. The psychiatric doctors, mostly all foreign physicians, would call us to see surgical problems, but we would also do examinations on various wards, male and female, and the pathology we uncovered was amazing: massive thyroids, breast cancers, huge hernias in men, and many incarcerated, lung cancers, and many others. A resident and a surgical intern were on call there all the time; we had excellent anesthesia, from the University nurse, Gertie Fife for one, and a corps of visiting doctors that were different from those we knew at Lakeside Hospital. I did a lot of

bizarre procedures there with the help of the visitants, like myotomies for achalasia of the esophagus, repairs of hiatal hernias, lobectomies for lung cancer, after diagnosis by bronchoscopies, thyroidectomies for obstructing goiter, emergency tracheostomies, multiple operations for breast cancers, multiple repairs of hip fractures and even a mastoidectomy for severe mastoiditis, an unheard of condition even then. At the request of the psychiatric doctors, we would get our entourage of intern, resident, and nurses to examine people in a given ward. When a surgical problem was uncovered, and there were many, we would have social services contact relatives for discussion and usually secondary permission to operate. If no relative could be contacted, the State would somehow verify our procedure. We developed a backlog of patients to be operated on, and many patients began to look forward to their procedures, for good or for bad. I guess you could say the program benefitted these poor sick individuals and it surely added to developing surgical skills of the trainees.

Pathology Service And Research:

Last but not least was the year we spent in the pathology department, six months in actual surgical pathology, cutting in the daily surgical specimens with the path resident, reading the microscopic slides, reporting and discussing results with surgeons. During this time, I did some three or four autopsies, all by myself with the help of path residents, presented findings at weekly conferences, and we had exposure to the big guns of pathology at the time: Howard Karsner, Harry Golblatt, Harold Orbison, to name a few. The day-to-day activity in the pathology department was far removed from the excitement of operative surgery, but for some unknown reason, I have always liked the concentration and cerebration required for each case and the visitants there were ever more demanding about detailed analysis of specimens. They made like a life was at stake. Dr. Karsner had published his worldwide acclaimed book on Pathology, Dr. Goldblatt was in progress with describing the connection between hypertension and kidney vascular occlusion, and Dr. Orbison was demonstrating, for the first time, the various plasma proteins in serum with electrophoresis. My six months in research was just down the hall, in this same atmosphere, and it will be detailed in the research chapter.

All this training activity for about five years was mixed in with repeated meetings, often with the heads of services, the chairman, residents above or below you, consisting of journal reviews, case reports, and trips to the library were high on the list of importance. I learned to love the Allen

Library, located right next to Lakeside Hospital, on the corner of Euclid Avenue and Adelbert Road, right across the avenue from Severance Hall, home of the Cleveland Orchestra. The library was old, quiet, had great smells of old books, an ancient copy of Andreas Versalius anatomy chart plus pictures of old famous surgeons on the walls. It had solid leather chairs and big oak tables in the reading room, which was reserved for residents and interns, and you could find every medical journal published in the whole world there. A huge winding staircase entrance greeted you; it was like going into your own quiet world for some little time, and I loved it.

Contrasted to the nice quiet studying in the library was the advanced resident's duty of presenting and speaking at meetings, and early on, when I returned from the military, one bad episode still persists in my subconscious mind: I got up to present a case in the main pathology amphitheater, row on row extending upward, filled with students, residents, visitants. I had a complete breakdown, was overcome, forgot my facts, can't remember what I said, finally rescued the presentation by foolishly reading my notes. But I knew then that if I was to advance at all, I would need help – so I enrolled in a downtown, Cleveland College speech course led by a fellow named Hantleman. It was scheduled once a week for six evenings, cost one hundred dollars, but I managed to work it in to a busy schedule. The instructor was one of the best practical teachers I'd ever known, taught us on the first day to grab any presentation available, do it bad or good, but just do it. He started us up front in a group; tell your name and what you do. There were policemen, firemen, lawyers, teachers in the group, and I was the only physician. Many important tricks were emphasized like talk to one or two people in a crowd, introduce with a subject to grab everyone's attention, keep speeches short – and many more. After this course, I sought out any presentation available, and enjoyed it, good or bad, to small or large audiences. Later on, my wife chided me for "never wanting to give up the microphone", and lots of my naivety and self esteem problems in front of large gatherings disappeared.

My time in training gave a basis for moving into the chance golden era of medical practice as a country surgeon, and in some way at the same time kept alive a yen for teaching and research, such as it was. A surgical practice without these two disciplines would be hard for me to imagine. These training years were also made more solid and enjoyable by a loving and cooperative wife, who shared the expectations of coming productive decades.

The Military:

My time in the military is difficult, almost ashamedly, for me to describe, because of the many men in my age group who were on the beach at Normandy while I was comfortably studying, getting room, board, and allowances as a PFC in the ASTP, the Army Specialized Training Program. We all could have been on this beach, possibly should have, but our rationalized thinking was the same as those in Washington, that it would be a long war and we ultimately would make our contribution.

On December 7, 1941, when the Japanese attack fell on Pearl Harbor, we heard of it on the radio at Mrs. Musser's rooming house in State College, Pa. We all thought that we should be doing something right away, like going down to enlist. My roommate, Francis Sullivan, the next day, a Monday, went down and signed up with the Navy V12 or V7 flight program. I was pending acceptance to medical school at Western Reserve, studying pre med courses, wondering what to do when war was declared on the axis powers – perhaps go enlist in something to avoid the upcoming draft? The government provided an answer when they promptly instituted a program to make bona-fide pre meds part of the MAC, the Medical Administrative Corps. We went to the ROTC Center at Penn State and were sworn in the service as 2nd Lieutenants, with no pay or allowances. This commission held until we were taken into the service again when the Army and Navy took over the med schools throughout the country, and made us all Pfc.'s, privates first class, with books and tuition paid, allowances for food and room, uniforms, all in a speed up program of three years – We all knew the planners in Washington were counting on a long war, and the need for doctors would be ever present in the military, even after the war, in civilian life.

We had daily roll calls, formations into squads, companies, and weekly maneuvers, games in fatigues. We made fun of our commander, Major Kaplin, a regular Army individual, not happy with his assignment, but all serious about the military. I guess you could say we were a select few, with potential value of some kind, in a chance time and place, studying pathology, physiology, pharmacology, while others were out there fighting and dying. All my close pals, Dick Watts, Jim Shumaker, Paul Ruth, eventually had active duty, acted the same, followed the combat activity of the war closely, but with mixed happy and depressed feelings, thinking we should be in it. This created a particular aggravation for me, with two brothers in combat units and my doctor Uncle Charlie killed on Okinawa. But my path was to finish with the hope to ultimately make a contribution.

Our induction into the Army was at Fort Hayes in Columbus, a two week session where we got uniforms, physical exams, and a lot of K-P duty, peeling potatoes and cleaning latrines because the regular Army guys hated these privileged students – and rightfully so. The physical exam doctor picked up my non-functioning right eye, and I had to sign a waiver to pass. I thought it pretty funny, my bad right eye got me through the years of high school and college sports, but a waiver was necessary to get me into the Army – I signed it right away!

Another comical thing happened with my psychiatric exam at Fort Hayes: The doctor asked me "did I ever have sexual intercourse"? And I naively replied; "you mean with a female?" He countered "with a male?" I'm sure he thought I was a strange fellow, never having had sexual intercourse, but he passed me anyhow! Thank you good doctor!

So, we finished Med School under these conditions, got a regular diploma, and our Army status continued into surgical training, but no more pay and allowances from the government. I had eighteen months of surgical training when my orders to MFSS (Medical Field Service School) were processed. They came with a real commission as a first Lieutenant in the AMC (Army Medical Corps) with the privilege to wear the gold caduceus on the left and the silver bar on the right side of our shirt collar. The feeling of pride over this was hard to suppress when confronting hometown folks like teachers, coaches and others when I was home on leave.

MFSS was in San Antonio, Texas, the home of the Alamo, and it was the place of my first excitement for possible things to come in the military: Fort Sam Houston was an old Army post, barracks with central squares for assembly, taps every night, revelry and flag raising every morning, fall out at 6:00 A.M. We learned about Army organization: medical battalions supporting divisions, platoon numbers, company formations, regiments, divisions. Desert maneuvers were frequent, setting up clearing and collecting stations. It was hot and I always got sick on the required salt tablets. All day lectures were about Army protocol, how and who to salute, where to get your pay. During the eight weeks there, like other soldiers, I had this nightly yearning for my dear wife, now with child, and during this time we exchanged lots of "hot letters" that we always shielded from our offspring at a later date.

The Great War was over, but there was still the expectation and mystery as to where would be your assignment. Korea was heating up. Japan was being occupied; Germany remained in chaos, the Soviet Union was still a threat. I was now a 3150D category, a surgical specialist with the authority to do any type of operation or head any unit in a medical battalion. I had visions of the strife, but welcomed surgical experience of a MASH unit or near combat assignment, but it never happened.

Nonetheless, there was uncertainly for one's future, a common prominent feature of where the bulletin board would spell out your assignment after graduation. So, we had my wife Dolly, with child, fly down to San Antonio for the affair. We skipped the ceremonies, but learned of our assignment to Fort Belvoir in Virginia, a POE for Europe, the Caribbean, Panama and South America. Part of the class went to the West Coast, POE for Korea, Asia, Japan and so on. We felt lucky, maybe going to Germany, and we spent a few great days, visiting with each other in Old San Antonio, with its interesting canals and the diminutive Alamo, before flying back to Cleveland.

At Fort Belvoir, the Army Engineering Center, I got quarters in the BOQ, but reported to the hospital and a Captain Taylor, whom I had known as an intern, was Chief of Surgery. He told me, in his office with a big sign on his desk, indicating he was the Chief, that there was no need for a surgeon here, and to not hang around the hospital. My assignment at Fort Belvoir was running daily sick call at the brig, which turned out to be a job that lasted about six months, ever filled with surprises.

The rumor circulated that we would be at Belvoir for at least six months before getting an overseas assignment, so my first order was to get my dear wife Dolly joining me. She was nearing term with our first child and living with her mother in Cleveland. It was courageous on her part, to leave the comfort and security of her mother's home for a venture into the tough confines of a strange military environment. I secured a one-room motel-apartment called Red Shutters, at fifty dollars ($50.00) a month, when a fellow doc told me of a vacancy. These places were at a premium about a quarter mile from the base. Our one-room abode was at the back, near the end of a long circular road, and our back yard bordered the Mount Vernon Estate of George Washington.

These were some of the best days that Dolly and I had together, influenced by our being apart, and by the feeling of not knowing where and when we would be going. I picked her up at the airport with a borrowed car; we went to the five and dime in Alexandria, bought pots, pans, knives and forks, our first housekeeping efforts to settle-in at "Red Shutters". Within a few weeks, she began labor and we went to the base hospital, a flat, one story, wooden structure, the same as all the buildings at the fort then, probably built for World War One.

We traveled to the hospital in the same borrowed car, owned by a fellow doc names Jones, from somewhere in the Midwest. The delivery was a drawn out contest: labor for several days, pain, big baby, thoughts of a section, but nobody there knew how to do one, possible ambulance to Walter Reed, but she finally delivered a 10½ pound baby boy. The Commanding General gave us a token prize at a small ceremony for producing the heaviest baby ever born at Fort Belvoir.

I continued in my important job of running the daily sick call at the brig. We had characters from all over the military in the Washington area, some fifty to one hundred strong, and they were frequently sick. I also got Tdy orders to do physical exams at the Army War College, and at Andrews Air Station, across the river with transportation, pay and allowances. These were fun because the candidates were interesting, different from my prisoners.

We moved to a ground level, two room apartment in the Washington suburb of Alexandria when Bob Thistlethwait, another doctor at the base, lived there and told us of the vacancy. You walked down a few cement steps to enter and the guy who owned the place was named Ratner, so we joked about calling it "Ratner's rat hole". We had several precious months there; Dolly interacted with other young military families, and we learned about how a good night's sleep could be ruined by crying offspring. The move to Alexandria, several miles from the fort, was also made possible by our acquiring a car, an old green Chevy, loaned to us by my Dad. This event allowed us repeated evening drives, with our new arrival in a basket on the back seat, about the Capitol and greater Washington, just across the river.

We were there in December when a snowstorm dumped about two inches of white on Washington, paralyzing the city for days.

Orders finally came for me to be transferred to the Panama Command and I had great visions of doing surgery at Gorgas Hospital. Dolly went back to Cleveland with our young son and my orders were to the POE in New Orleans, Camp Leroy Johnson on Lake Ponchetrane. I arrived in New Orleans by train on a Sunday night; Mardi Gras was in its last day, hotels were filled, and they all laughed at me when I applied for a one-night room. I settled for a flophouse, slept all night with my loaded pistol under the pillow. In the morning I inquired for the whereabouts of Camp Leroy Johnson and they told me it was at the end of the line, to take a streetcar named Desire! The guard at the base gate told me that I should have called and they would have sent a car to pick me up at the railroad station. It was my first indication – and many more in the military, whereby Doc officers had special privileges. We got great quarters in the BOQ and the rumor was that we would be on our way, by troop ship in a week or two.

However, in the military, screw-ups happen inadvertently, chance factors are common due to the complex nature of affairs. The first: Our troop ship ran aground and got stuck in the mud on entering the port of New Orleans and a special vessel necessary to get it free was coming through the canal. We would be detained at Camp Leroy Johnson for about six weeks instead of one.

Those six weeks produced some of the most fascinating times of my whole military experience. There were about twenty officers in the group, and I got to know them all! One friend later became a colleague, Bill Geller, trained as an Internist in Boston. George Renault was an artillery officer, chaplains, infantry, and pilots, all going to the Caribbean, Panama, or South America. Bill Geller and I went to the base hospital, asked if we could help with anything, and we got the "go away" treatment. Many of the line officers came from combat duty in Germany; their daily routine started with a shot of whiskey and cigarette. Their afternoon poker games had five hundred dollars changing hands like dimes or quarters, and they were still "smokin' and drinkin'". In groups, we often rode the streetcar Desire to the French Quarter and Bourbon Street, all acquiring our favorite performers there, dancers and strippers. I learned, in amazement, about how some of these girls developed muscles in their pelves to pick up half dollar coins and dollar bills off the surface of bars and tables.

In typical Army fashion, one night-morning, about 2:00 A.M., a Sergeant woke us up, said: "Pack your bags, we're leaving". A bus took us to the air base at Biloxi, Mississippi, where we sat around for hours 'til the fog lifted, got on a plane and took off for parts unknown. We landed in Panama; it was hot and humid. The Commander at the HQ there informed us that no doctors were needed, and next another plane to San Juan, Puerto Rico. From there, my final assignment was to Losey Field, a military post on the Southwestern part of the island.

It was a rigid Army installation with a West Point Colonel as Commander. There were weekly drills and parades, which I tried to avoid but couldn't. The mission was to produce combat ready units, one was a cav-recon outfit, came from Germany, with a Captain Commander, Van Lentin, a fellow that I played baseball with at Penn State –a small world! They took me, on a half-track, with them on several maneuvers, wanted me to play catcher on their post baseball team, but I refused. Being the last doctor to arrive on the base, there was one other, I got appointed V-D officer. Venereal disease was a problem. We lectured and showed grotesque films once a week, to little avail. Would you believe part of this job was to inspect the houses of prostitution in Ponce, a near-by town, for cleanliness and neatness, as if these features could make a difference!

There was a small hospital on the base with a nurse and a few corpsmen, an x-ray unit and laboratory. We did minor surgery, sick call for soldiers, dependents, and native workers. I remember seeing my first case of Choriocarcinoma there in the wife of a fellow Puerto Rican officer. I couldn't believe her pelvic mass after a spontaneous abortion. We sent her to specialists in San Juan, but she eventually died. We all went to the funeral; they were friends and we were all saddened.

There was housing on the base for dependents but the waiting list was long, you had to put in your name, wait your turn, and finally Dolly with our first-born flew into San Juan from New York. We had a treasured meeting the night after her arrival, but the next day, a scary flight over mountains in a C47 to the airstrip at Losey Field. We changed quarters several times there, finally ending side-by-side with Don O'Connor, the other medical officer, married to Lolita, a great looking Spanish girl, Puerto Rican, whose father owned the Pharmacy Le Fe in San Juan. We got to be super friends with them.

A traumatic event, never to be forgotten, when one day Dolly called me at the hospital, and I came home to find our son James, crawling about the floor, screaming in pain. He had an incarcerated inguinal hernia that I was no way going to operate on, so we held up the mail C47, rushed us to San Juan, then an ambulance to Rodriguez General Hospital, the center of medicine for the Caribbean Command. The major O.D. at admissions, smoking a cigarette, with his feet up on his desk, told us: There was no one assigned to his hospital that could repair a baby hernia, but we could get a Puerto-Rican civilian surgeon to see him in the morning!? Meanwhile we got the kid into a bed at the hospital and he suddenly stopped crying. By chance, the hernia spontaneously reduced. The specialist from San Juan, a Dr. Pasalaqua, saw him the next day, but there was no need for an emergency operation. The situation could have had a fatal outcome, but we were lucky. Our visit at the hospital lasted a few days enjoying the base movies and food before returning to Losey Field. The pattern reminded me of what transpired later when I visited a civilian hospital at Auqadilla, a town near the air base at Ramey. Casualties of all kinds, fractures, abdominal and chest trauma, incurred on Friday, Saturday or Sunday would all be placed in a temporary holding area to take turns, for operations on Monday. Surgeons would come, sometimes from San Juan, and do the best they could.

We got a pleasant, unexpected transfer to the Army Air Base at Ramey when a surgeon, Capt. Sanford, went back to the States. Bill Geller, my friend from the days at Camp Leroy Johnson, was the established Chief of Medicine at Ramey, and he put in a good word for us. The base had a fifty-bed hospital with operating rooms, obstetrical area, clinic facilities, nurses and nurse anesthesia. We served people from a busy facility at that time, with planes flying the Berlin Airlift, GHQ for the Caribbean Command, also the HQ for Air Sea Rescue in the South Atlantic. The base was located on Borinquen point, an out-jutting portion of the island that marked the division of the Atlantic Ocean with the Caribbean Sea. We got quarters in a stilted wooden house, overlooking the ocean. The streets on the base were lined with palm trees; ocean breezes were the rule.

The base was widely known in the military as the "Country Club of the Caribbean", rivaled only by duty at Hickam Field in Hawaii. We had numerous generals and high ranking government officials assigned to Ramey for Tdy, temporary duty, and I got to operate on many of them - mostly hernias, peri rectal troubles, and a few appendectomies. I can still feel the thrill and the anxiety of doing my first appendectomy there, in a young soldier, with nurse anesthesia, corpsmen assisting, a great relief when he recovered. It was there that I learned to do a lot of section surgery, helping Don O'Connor, our OB and GYN Chief, also transferred from Losey Field. We acquired a good reputation with dependents throughout the whole Caribbean command, all the islands, and even those from San Juan. There was also a big civilian practice from workers on the base.

One case, outstanding in my memory, etched in my mind, was about one night at the hospital, I was O.D. on call, and a child came in with croup-laryngeal obstruction. He had all the signs, suprasternal retraction, apprehension but was lapsing into depression. We did an emergency tracheostomy and saved a life. The kid's Dad was a Colonel with a high rank for flight administration on the base, and he eventually helped me to get a flight back to the States for discharge in time to resume my surgical training.

Along with the active surgical experience at Ramey, which may have been partial payback to the service for the free education afforded me, there were many additional features of our life there. One was the interesting visit's to the doctors and hospital in the neighboring town of Aquadilla, giving them some of our antibiotics and other supplies that they were solely lacking. Short on simple innovations like screens on the windows above ground levels and sheets on stained bare mattresses in the pediatric wards, children were near death. It was a series of desperate scenes there, in contrast to what we had in our base hospital. Our corpsmen helped to get some of these supplies, and I learned a bit about the underground workings of military supply lines with my Aides Harry, Nelson, and Bud Cunningham. Nelson and Bud were Sergeants, called me Captain Governor, always made sure there were new tires on my jeep, and we had our refrigerator stocked with food when we returned from a trip as ship's doctor.

The boys were examples of the good and the bad. The bad being when they borrowed my jeep, went with it to an off-limits place in Aquadilla, got chased by MP's, got away by going across sugar cane fields, and my license number was recognized. The MP's came to my office, never accused me; the boys were lucky, I got them off with only a few days in the brig.

We now lived in a solid, low, stone and brick house, hurricane proof, with a lime tree in the back yard. Dolly won a big barrel of Don Q rum in a lottery at the Officers Club, which was situated overlooking the beautiful Caribbean Sea. Like all the other folks, we had a Puerto Rican maid, Aleaha, and many friends like a hospital worker, Maria Medina, who became the Godmother of our second born, Charles Timothy. His delivery was helped along smoothly by a fellow doctor, Chuck Novey, who delayed his return to the States as a favor to us.

The months passed quickly in this "ideal time of life" for us that in retrospect, was full of new and exciting challenges. We were young and eager – the prevailing idea then was for doctors to get out of the military. Conversely, the new Air Force had a campaign on to recruit doctors and they offered me a majority and other perks to stay in the service, but my desire to get board certification at the University in Cleveland overshadowed the apparent easier road. Who knows what could have been on the "path not taken"?

So, Dolly returned to the States on a Pan Am flight from San Juan to New York with two babies, nursing busy Timmy, and under the watchful eye of a fellow soldier, a Sergeant, who said he'd care for them on the flight. Her mother met the plane in New York, but Dolly had the uneasy task of staying with my relatives in Pennsylvania until I was discharged. It took about six weeks for me to get a flight out of Ramey, helped by the Colonel whose son I had operated on, a B53 from Ramey to Camp Leroy Johnson in Louisiana. Then, after a few days, I caught a ride on a C45 to Olmstead Air Base, near Harrisburg Pa. After a few days of nervously worrying about getting to my resident position, discharge papers were produced. I collected my pay, and a day later became a civilian.

We made it back to Cleveland a day or two early for me to start a 3rd year residency at University Hospitals. Don't think for a moment that I would ever forget the sacrifices of untold numbers of soldiers that made my time in the military a safe passage.

How We Came To Country Surgery:

The string of chance events that led to our placement in rural Union County is long and complex, but the terminal circumstances are interesting: It was 1952; the Korean War, started in 1950 was still on, physicians were being drafted and preparing for a continued conflict, and my military service was over. A fellow resident in surgical training with me, one Bob Foreman, had just received a letter from his draft board to report for active duty. This same fellow, as luck would have it, was turned down for Army enlistment when the military took over our medical school, because he stuttered, but I guess stuttering was no longer a reason to be barred from military service, especially with the increasing demand for physicians in Korea. We were both, along with several other doctors, finishing our 4th year of surgical training, getting ready to embark somewhere, probably practice.

One day he came into my resident dorm room and said: "J-J-J-Jim-Jimmy there's a place in Union County with a new hospital and they need a general surgeon. I have been d-d-down there, there's a house, and it's a good deal, and I can't go." This was the first I ever heard of Union County Memorial. Before this, we were corresponding with a Clinic in Great Falls, Montana, one in Johannesburg, South Africa, we visited Palmerton, Pennsylvania, where the main industry was a zinc mill, and we contacted the Karolinski Institute in Sweden, where I had a chance for an Eleanor Roosevelt scholarship because of my research time in Dr. Leuchtenberger's Laboratory. This would have paid us $3000 per year along with travel expenses.

However, we followed Bob Foreman's advice and visited Union County and Columbus, Ohio. The latter to obtain the impression of Dr. Zollinger, the Chief of Surgery at Ohio State University. He told me he would give me a Clinical Faculty appointment at Ohio State, that Union County was a great place, but: "I'm not sending any of my residents there." Despite this strange response, we drove up Route 33 to Marysville from Columbus, and we were impressed with how small this town, the County Seat of Union County, was. It had a big courthouse, and a small, new Memorial Hospital that was about one-year-old. The center of town had a bank on one corner, an old hotel across the street, a pool hall and a jewelry store, and a downtown A&P, and McAuliffe's hardware store nearby. Just down the street was the fire department garage, also housing the emergency squad vehicle and it's volunteer members that I would come to know well.

The hospital had thirty beds, ten for obstetrics and twenty for medicine and surgery. There were some ten general practice physicians sending their patients there, two of the doctors were from Plain City, with a near-by Amish community, and one very busy physician, Dr. Burt, in Milford Center, a five mile removed farming and railroad community. Surgery was being done on an itinerant basis by visiting practitioners from locations in Columbus and Delaware. My initial impression from the then Chief of Staff, Dr. Fred Callaway (said to be a descendant of Daniel Boone), other prominent physicians, Administrator, Board President P.C. Williams (also the director of Scott's Seed, a prominent local company) were positive. I remember travelling to Plain City, meeting Dr. Karrer in a local schoolroom where he was doing athletic exams. He was a plain speaking, confident doctor that told me I would do well here if my work was standard, caring and continuous. Dr. Dana Morey, a local philanthropist, in conjunction with Scott's Seed, offered us a loan of $5000 to move my family and begin practice.

The enthusiasm over our coming to Memorial, the concept of raising our family in a rural setting, yet the proximity with advantages of Metropolitan Columbus, and probability of a faculty appointment at Ohio State made us decide to cast our lot in Marysville. Not to mention that we were running out of funds saved from my Captain's pay and our stipend at that time as $150.00 per month from University Hospitals of Cleveland.

Memorial Hospital Of Union County

The Early Days And Beyond:

A farmer's field encircled by a small creek, donated to an enterprising group of individuals called a hospital association, and Memorial Hospital was founded. It was a county endeavor, like perhaps hundreds of others in the late nineteen forties and early fifties, when funds were raised, time was donated to produce many county hospitals, like those in surrounding towns of London, Washington Courthouse, Urbana, Lima, and others in Ohio. A few decades later when the American College of Surgeons released some of their statistics on total operations performed, those in small county hospitals far outnumbered their counterparts in big city academic institutions. The surgery in these small hospitals was being done by individuals with varied experience, some itinerant, many returning from the military, and many with training similar to my own. Fortunately for us, at Memorial Hospital of Union County, Malcolm MacIvor, a local general practitioner at that time, also a Naval veteran, who had interned at St. Lukes Hospital in Cleveland, brought to our hospital board a concept from that institution, about how surgery should be done only by people with Board Qualified training. This was then a new perception for authorities in many small hospitals, and as we shall see, a notion for instigating a considerable number of complex legal conflicts (see chapter on legal entanglements).

Memorial was about one year old when we came in 1953, comprised of thirty beds, twenty for medicine and surgery, ten for obstetrics, wherein all the deliveries were being done by general practice physicians. A single operating room, emergency room, lab and x-ray facilities were also present. The Administrator was one, Francis Helmick, a great lady, a nurse, who was recruited from the London, Ohio hospital by P.C. Williams, then President of the local Scott Seed Company, also hospital board chairman. Francis was still active at the time of this writing, ninety years of age, even though she lost a few years from stress of legal problems with physicians in the early years. After her tour of duty at Memorial, she continued to contribute in the medical field by leading Ohio and American Cancer Societies.

Technical duties in the Lab and X-ray, an integral section of our hospital, were handled by two young people, Frank Cossu and Dean Thogmorton (he never wanted to be called Throgmorton). They did all the lab work: counts of red cells, white blood cells and urine exams then relatively simple, but there were no fancy machines, so they struggled with the chemistry for blood sugars, blood urea nitrogens, even blood Ph and carbon dioxides. Doctors ordered few bacterial cultures then, but more important, these two technicians did the typing for our blood transfusions. You'll never believe this, but those two guys also took all the x-rays, mostly upright chest and abdominal films, along with fracture pictures of all types. There was only one general practice doctor that ordered and could read EKGs (electrocardiograms), but these along with BMRs (basal metabolic rates to evaluate thyroid disease) they also encompassed.

I love to tell the story of how I usually gave lab and x-ray people presents at Christmas time, usually candy or some small gift. One time I bought a case of good wine, and while waiting several weeks to give it to all, we consumed it ourselves! However, in the years when we first arrived, and there were two people doing the work, I gave two or three gifts, but some forty years later, I had to give fifteen to laboratory people and eighteen to x-ray personnel. You might say that these two fellows initially did the same work as about thirty people with comparable results?

Laboratory activities and evaluating tissue removed at surgery are components of the Pathology Department, an essential unit of any hospital. We were fortunate to have one, Emrick Von Haam, a world-renowned member of the field. He digressed from his busy activities at Ohio State, where he was chairman of the department, with teaching and research responsibilities, to give us time and a separate arrangement for our institution, financial as well as academic. Dr.Von Haam was a German fellow, all the way, Austrian, with neatly trimmed mustache, impressive looking in an academic way, always bowed and clicked heels when introduced to ladies, often kissed their hand. This delighted many local doctors' wives. He once reminded me, when we were discussing a local school levy issue about our school being twenty years old, that his school in Austria was two hundred years old and was still functioning well. I had this "yen" to get my name in the medical literature with Doctor Van Haam, for what reason I'll never know, probably ego gratification, and I worked hard, measuring immune cells in appendices from individuals of various ages. We got it accepted as a letter to the editor in the American Journal of Pathology, about 1960. I considered it a triumph for a surgeon to get any kind of a publication in a Path Journal, but you know, with all the others, it's turning to dust on library shelves now.

The research effort of the Pathology Department at the University then was extensive and significant, mostly delving into cervical cancer, but they also published widely on wound healing in diabetes. An associate, Dr. Dante Scarpelli and the Chief contributed to describing changes in the uterine cervix cells from normal through pre-malignant to frank cancer. I had a great many "bull sessions" with Dante about research and philosophy in the old days, and I "name dropped" many times when Dr. Scarpelli became the Head of Pathology at Northwestern University in Chicago. When one gets old and has been around for a long time, one tends to "name drop" often as in this book, but one also gets a long look at how fleeting fame can be: Dr. Von Haam was always consulted by surgery, medicine, always sat up front with presenters at meetings, laughed and joked with everyone, had the ultimate and final say about most problems. But twenty years later, when he was retired, I remember seeing him, when I was entering a big meeting at his University, he was on his way to the bathroom, bent over, walking with difficulty, and I was the only one who recognized him to say hello. He hardly knew me.

And for our hospital in the first decade, he would travel one evening a month to present a slide show of our most interesting surgical cases. These meetings were well attended especially when free dinner was offered with the meeting. I guess you could say that this was our initial association with the University that gave our hospital a huge advantage in education of physicians, long before the accumulation of education credits became mandatory. Foreseeing the need for these credits to be demanded by the AMA and other authorities, and more important to keep us aware of medical advances, we instituted monthly meetings whereby our own doctors led discussions on topics like anemia, antibiotics, diabetes and others. At first we were granted category one credit for these gatherings, but after a year or so, the OSMA came up with the idea that we had to pay some outside associate to come and supervise these sessions. We complained but to no avail. It was the beginning of "pay for education credits" in our complex random world, necessary for progress no doubt.

One of the problems in the early days was acquiring frozen sections: we had to schedule them a few days in advance to get the pathologist in-house during our operation, mostly for breast masses, but other contingencies arose. A frozen section was a procedure of immeasurable help to the surgeon. A piece of tissue from a mass is removed, quickly frozen, sectioned with a microtome, stained, and a diagnosis read from a glass slide in perhaps ten to fifteen minutes. It was particularly helpful in the sometime perplexing situation when, with gross observation, one had difficulty identifying a process as bizarre inflammation, lymphoma, or carcinoma, the former two conditions being better treated with medicine or perhaps radiation, while the latter would require more extensive operation. We "tinkered around" with many ideas for getting quick frozen sections, even one "crazy idea" to use carrier pigeons, but we finally got the hospital to provide us with a swift courier by automobile. There were times when I did my own frozen sections, take the biopsy, drop out of the operation, section tissue, stain, read it, and come back in, lots of stress associated with this solution. Perhaps this action was the basis for a recurring horrible dream that I had years after retiring; whereby I would leave an operation before finishing, and for bizarre or unknown reasons, not return.

At sometime in the early 1970's we acquired a private practice pathologist that divided his time between our hospital and other local towns, but eventually our administrators arrived at a contract with the University again, resulting in political and/or financial arrangements for their sending one individual to reside in our hospital. It was a joy to have this on-site fellow directing our laboratory, doing frozen section, and being there for discussions about patients and directing weekly conferences. Medical practice was getting more complicated, our patient load was increasing, other specialists began to appear, and many staff members continued to support our association with the University. Bacterial resistance to antibiotics was an increasing dilemma, essential laboratory tests were increasing by "leaps and bounds", connection to the medical world outside the county was top priority for acquiring world-class expertise. Few patients in surrounding towns, no patients in-hospital knew of this non-advertised advantage to their care that was started then and still exists today.

One of the main reasons we came to Union County was the prospect of my getting a clinical faculty appointment at Ohio State University from Dr. Zollinger, the chief of surgery there. My initial positive expectations of this designation were borne out in that it served me well through the years. Not only did it allow me to attend multiple conferences like M & M (morbidity and mortality), contribute to Saturday morning surgical rounds, have sessions with bright young students on a five to one basis weekly – and all this for a $100.00 yearly parking ticket. Not to mention tickets to home football games and membership in the OSU faculty club for $35.00 per month, where my family had a goodly number of great dinners, even meeting Woody Hayes, the famous football coach at one of his lectures there. Furthermore, I had a unique position at the University, being an "outsider looking in", exempt from politics and financial diversions in the department, not "bucking for corporal", an old army term for seeking advancement, as I remained a clinical instructor for some forty years. One comment from Dr. Zollinger, when we first met, confused me a little bit: he said "The hospital there is a great place, but you notice I'm not sending any of my residents to apply". Later on I knew why this statement became an important topic in my chapter on legal entanglements.

As mentioned, I noted many staff members in favor of our association with the University but others objecting to this influence was difficult for me to understand. Perhaps there was a feeling of infringement on their practice, patient-wise or financial, but I never imagined until later that it could be related to legal entanglements. But nevertheless there were definite objections, and the most ardent came from Dr. H.E. Stricker, a very busy practitioner. H.E., as I always called him, would say to me: "Jim, don't waste your time down there, we need you here". He would frequently have me paged at University Hospital for some minor local emergency of no consequence. No way would I think that one reason for his aversion to Ohio State was his love for his medical school alma mater, The University of Michigan, also the archrival of the Buckeyes in football. He had a huge following of devoted patients, nearly all of them delivered by him, and he was also the main medical director of our local Marysville Reformatory for Women, one of several State prisons. H.E. treated me like a son when we first came to town, introduced me to his barber, bank tellers, insurance agent, and took me to the Reformatory to meet Mrs. Ma Riley, the warden.

Ma weighed about three hundred pounds, sat on a high throne to meet me, with a wide, white flowing dress, and I was fortunate she granted me the blessing of doing the surgery on her girls, for which I was hoping to get at that time, the arrangement lasting for some 20 years until political change terminated it. But you can't believe the cases we saw there: swallowed pins, razor blades, pencils, pelvic abscesses, drug problems with knife wounds, slashed wrists, breast masses, thyroid cancers, mesenteric infarction, hepatitis A&B and our first case of "flesh eating bacteria", necrotizing fasciitis, that ended in multiple amputations and death. Ma Riley was innovative in many ways. She had set up a small hospital, a well-equipped operating room, staffed with some of her favorite girls, and our team always got super royal treatment when we came with our nurses, anesthesia, and packs to operate. We did many routine procedures there but took the bigger ones like massive fibroids and radical breasts to Memorial about one mile away. A comment about the women from the Reformatory that we operated on: They all required a guard, never gave us trouble, they were always appreciative and occasionally their relatives would come and visit, usually cooperative and understanding.

H.E. handled the doctoring at the Reformatory with concerned efficiency: he was a maverick in many ways, and I wrote a poem about this aspect of his personality. Never did he believe in attending medical meetings, always against rules and regulations set out by insurance payers, gambling for large sums of money was on his agenda on many Saturday nights, and a hobby of wireless radio connected him to people all around the world. He repeatedly called me to operate on patients with questionable indications, which I was always refusing, but now and then he was right (see cases of human interest). One of many comical incidents with him occurred when one afternoon he walked around my house, knocked on the window when I was in bed with my wife, it was a real emergency; I scrambled out of bed and went to the hospital to care for a bleeding lady. Whenever I came back into town from a meeting or a small vacation, he was usually the first one to call – but what more could a surgeon ask for, to be so notable and in demand; these were great days!

The general practice doctors usually assisted on complex surgical cases, each had his unique performance: Dr. Karrer and Dr. Paul Zaugg were the best; they were interested in the surgery and the former was always concerned with his patients welfare, always stayed to the end so he could go and talk to the family. Dr. MacIvor was good for about one hour, then he would start tapping instruments on the drapes, indicating boredom, and he would leave, being replaced fortunately by a nurse. Dr. Burt would come in for about thirty minutes, once in a while get weak, once passed out because of the anti-hypertensive medicine he was taking. The older doctors never assisted; we had great nurses and we actually trained individuals, high school and college students to be excellent assistants in the operating room. Many of these people went on to medical school and became great doctors, Harry Reynolds for one, became Chief of Colo-Rectal surgery at Western Reserve, and four or five other became notable physicians. Rickie Timmins became an invasive cardiologist, Susan Anderson ended as the Dean of Seton Hall Medical School in New Jersey. There were few restrictions on young people being trained in our operating room. We had one young man just out of high school, had minor trouble with the law, the nurses and I trained, became one of our best assistants for many years, did everything about the operating room, moved patients, instrument nurse, surgical assistant. Some of the nurses objected to this policy but it was a matter of suitability at the time.

An Initial Scary Proposition Anesthesia:

I lost many a night's sleep over this discipline in the early days, a consistent problem, no reliable source of individuals providing safe performance, contrary to conditions in my training and in the military, where competence was assumed. It was common practice in the hospital for one practitioner, Fred Calloway, to do tonsillectomies with drop ether. I did some of these myself in the first few years, and I learned that drop ether, not ideal for comfort, but with a wide margin of safety, was the best bet for general anesthesia administered by the patient's doctor. We did a lot of cases with locally injected agents like Novocain and Procaine, nerve blocks and field blocks, with standing by local doctors administering intravenous sodium pentothal, the latter a scary maneuver since I was the only one with endotracheal tube experience. I usually gave my own spinal anesthesia since part of my surgical training at Reserve, with nurse anesthetists, was my inserting the needle between vertebrae. I was known as the guy to call, and I had a reputation: There was "never a spinal canal that I could not enter". Spinal anesthesia worked well for lower extremity, anal and lower abdominal work, often supplemented with narcotics like morphine; the tremendous value of this drug in shock states and pain was known to me from way back. You can see why I constantly worried about this essential component of surgical care, sometimes turning patients away because we lacked this expertise, but we were lucky, we never lost a patient, nor had a near catastrophe during these years.

Good fortune smiled on us when we met Dr. Chester Theiss, a doctor from the neighboring town of Delaware, who had some training in anesthesia. He had worked in our hospital with the itinerant surgeon Dr. Ed Jenkins, and he agreed to devote some time from his busy schedule to help me with selected surgeries. After a while, he spent more and more time with us, and it was a pleasure to rely on his skill with endotracheal tubes and gas machines with closed systems. Eventually, Chester would come over when we called, slide his bag across the slippery OR floor and begin. We did many tough cases for a few good years but he went on to get advanced training at the University that led him to the professorship in anesthesia at the University of Tennessee. We were proud to have worked with him, and the OR girls missed their "jumping with joy" when he would arrive to do a case.

The whole specialty of anesthesia was in flux about the time I finished training and journeyed into practice. The controversy at Western Reserve, probably the same in many institutions about the country, centered around the role of nurses in the profession, whether or not they should be authoritative and in charge of patient's welfare at the head of the table, or should this be under the supervision of a physician? The latter situation prevailed, but ultimately nurses and physicians assumed their own levels of training and proficiency. In my early residency and in the military, nurses administered most anesthetics, but the surgeon sometimes was the boss. One example at University Hospitals of Cleveland was a strong willed, big lady, a nurse, Gertie Fife, "ruled the roost." She was always outspoken in Saturday morning rounds, often denouncing the value of endotracheal tubes, citing their irritative characteristics especially in thyroid operations. To her credit, in those days, endotracheal tubes were big, red rubber, and unwieldy; while the oral airway was the standard and easily inserted. Gertie was moved aside when Bill Holden took over from Carl Lenhart as Chief of Surgery, and a great, red headed young physician, Ham Davis, became department chairman to deal with the ever-expanding demands of more modern anesthesia.

Competent Anesthesia, Thank The Lord!

Fortunately for us, at Memorial several of our young doctors enrolled in a course sponsored by the Chairman of the department at OSU, one J. Jacoby, M.D., a perfect fit for anesthesia, a saint type man gently spoken, caring, confident, and with a yen for teaching. He knew there was a need for good anesthesia outside big city centers, and he was willing to give some of himself to training people for work out in the counties. The story of these two doctors that devoted six months of their lives for daily treks to the city for training reads like a novel, each one with lots of good and a little bad. They were both part of the surgical scheme for many years after Dr. Theiss left, both now long deceased, part of another time and place, like all of us were.

The first was Dr. Robert Fuller, a graduate of Ohio State, an ardent alumnus, eager and well equipped to handle any problem in anesthesia, all with competence through the years in the many hundreds of cases we did together. However, there were a few Monday mornings when I would have to go to his house, get him out of bed so we could start the eight o'clock case. This was usually frustrating for the referring physician, who was waiting to assist with surgery. I was always on the brink of saying "Bob, you'll have to improve or we'll get someone else", but I never would say this before starting the case, for fear of influencing his work. Then, when the operation was successfully over, when we were through the stress together, I could never bring myself to criticize - until the next similar happening for me to repeat the process. Bob was always a jovial fellow. One of his favorite sayings, in response to the greeting "How's it going, Bob", was "It don't go, you gotta push it". He told my wife that she had "sexy toes" one time when she was sun bathing. Now and then he would drop by my house in the morning or afternoon for a shot of our best Irish whiskey when he was not on call. His wife was one of those smart ladies, but a near idiot in our minds, always had dirty dishes in the sink when I came by of mornings, and often giving out crude and obtrusive statements. One time she asked my wife if I had some objection to our children being raised Catholic and my wife's reply was "He only wanted the best for his children", pretty clever for a quick response?

Weekends at his old alma mater, that he enjoyed so much, eventually ended his career. Coming back from these gatherings he had several car accidents, the first resulted in a broken leg but the second was fatal in the strangest way: he was brought to our emergency room by the squad one night, after he ran off the road from route 33 and hit a tree. A few chest pains were thought to be rib fractures, but there was a strange widening of the mediastinal shadow on his chest film. When I saw him on afternoon rounds, he was in shock and he told me "Jim, I have no feeling in my legs". We all rushed to University Hospital, he went right to surgery, in a bathtub of ice water for hypotension, and Dr. Howard Sirak was the thoracic consultant. I helped, we opened the chest to find a large mediastinal hematoma, it ruptured immediately and the massive hemorrhage that followed could not be replenished by transfusion. He died on the table. We were devastated. There was no way we could describe the grief and sadness of that night. His problem was a torn aortic arch, several similar cases were described later as associated with seat belts, and for repair the then not known procedure, cardiac by-pass was necessary. He had a great family, his parents were from Cleveland, sacrificed a lot to assist him through medical school, visited us many times. His dad gave me a customized golf driver one time for a Christmas gift.

Mae Zaugg, M.D. was also one of our significant anesthesia people. (I hate to use the term provider, it's too modern). She was a girl ahead of her time, as a graduate of Oho State as well. There were several great things I remember about Mae, one was that she loved several Siamese cats that were not always happy with you when you visited. The other was an outstanding postulate she issued at staff meetings, and as time went on I have copied it many times: "It's the same play with different actors," referring to the same in-hospital problems that come up year after year. I'm sure she copied it from Shakespeare or somewhere, but it always rang true in later years as controversy repeated itself. She married Paul Zaugg, another physician, for what reason I don't know; they had a joint practice in town with a big house on a prominent corner. However, they had an offspring, one Cindy that was brain damaged at birth, perhaps cerebral palsy. This being a burden prompted Mae to abandon her role as a practicing doctor, and fortunately for us, she took Dr. Jacoby's course in anesthesia. She was slow moving but completely competent, allowing us to have numerable long, tedious cases with safety, cautious but thorough, having no trouble taking on the toughest situations, and we had many. Eventually she gave up working, and retired to take care of her dependent daughter and care for her husband, Dr. Paul, who was always coming up with some strange disease. One incident illustrates what a "spunky" character she was: Her husband was on the G. U. service (Genitourinary service) at University Hospital where he had a lymph node dissection and chemotherapy. He was there for several weeks, not doing well, getting worse daily. In the middle of one night, she rented an ambulance, signed him out, and brought him to Memorial. We opened a massive retroperitoneal abscess and he got better rapidly. We were all happy this situation ended pleasantly.

Random Events To Our Advantage:

To emphasize how chance and randomness influences events, our next good fortune in anesthesia was to get Carolyn Ziegler and her husband John. Carolyn was another female way ahead of her time, professor at Ohio State, prominent in student teaching, reminded me and Malcolm MacIvor of a British Sergeant Major with an underarm riding crop. She was in line to become the Chief of Anesthesia at the University, but Dr. Zollinger, Chairman of Surgery was prejudiced and hated women in medicine; so he made sure the position went to Dr. Hammelburg, a male faculty member. Carolyn got angry and left. After a short stint at the University of Pittsburgh, she and her husband decided to go "country living", bought a home along the river outside of town, and they came to Memorial, giving us world-class anesthesia. Her husband John, much subjugated in their relationship, was also a PhD in chemistry, giving him a part time job at Scotts' Seed investigating toxic products. He was also an M.D., had his Boards in anesthesia, liked classical music, a true academic type, timid, in contrast to his wife Carolyn. Late in his tenure with us, he developed a mass in the parotid gland region that we thought was a mixed tumor, but we removed it to find it was actually Hodgkin's lymphoma. Ten years later he succumbed to this disease.

My relationships with Carolyn were not always sweet or smooth, but for the most part, I think we respected each other a lot. Differences would sometimes arise with regards to our decisions for operating on some patient with high-risk status, and rarely I would have to evoke my old saying: "We'll get someone else to do it", she would eventually go along reluctantly. We never had an operating room death with any of these elective cases. Arguments would occur over simpler things, like signing pre-op physical exams. Even though I knew most of my patients and often their families personally, the hospital had rules about patients going to surgery had to have a signed physical exam, preferentially by their doctor, alerting anesthesia about things like heart disease, previous surgery, diabetes, and others. When we acquired specialists of internal medicine, respiratory or cardiac, we always tried to have one available when we did high-risk patients, but Carolyn would not start without that signature. She was right; often I would sign the form myself to keep her happy.

Another "Chance" Advantage:

Carolyn acquired Dr. Ben Hoagland, a dentist, to assist in the anesthesia department when things got too busy for her and John to handle. To say Benjie Hoagland was a great guy would be the "understatement of the day". In my mind he was an exceptional anesthesiologist, fitting right in with everybody in the operating room scene, nurses, doctors, aides and patients. His training was at various hospitals; Riverside and University, even once went to Mexico to learn about a new technique for obstetrical anesthesia. As time went on Carolyn retired and a few other people were hired, but whenever we had a high-risk or difficult case coming up, I would insist on Benjie doing the anesthesia for my patient. He had a "knack" for making difficult situations look easy, rapid inductions, simple tube insertions, intravenous lines quickly established, all these plus intelligent banter during the procedure. Several new people were recruited by Carolyn before she retired, but the hospital administration moved into the "doctor recruiting business" and they hired several other people, all good, but none gave me the feeling of competence that I had with Carolyn, Benjie, or even the past general practice doctors, Mae Zaugg or Bob Fuller. However, eventually the hospital authorities made a good move by hiring Shelia.

How Can The Good And Bad Develop?

Shelia was an Indian girl, trained at the University of Chicago, worked at Cook County Hospital, the American center of shocking surgical problems. She could do everything, including go to the ICU and place a Swan-Ganz catheter, a real trick to float the balloon end through the pulmonary artery to rest in small vessels at the lung periphery and record pressure variations, extremely helpful in any shock situation. She came to town in the mid eighties or so, bought a house on the periphery of our local golf course, and she was designated Chief of Anesthesia by the administration. Now, here's where I apply my general philosophical edict that most everything and everybody has good and bad features, depending on "your frame of mind". Shelia, the administrator, most of the hospital board members, had a vision for the future of anesthesia at Memorial. Shelia's plan was to employ two or three nurse anesthetists, supervise them while they were working in various rooms, for then we had four operating rooms rather than two, and as we'll discuss later, a mixture of specialists operating almost every day. However, the plan was disrupted by Dr. Hoagland's desire not to retire, and further, a few surgeons, including me and the ophthalmologist, along with some patients, would request Benjie to do their anesthesia. This mixed up situation went on for many months, but there was never any hazard for patients; both camps were perfectly reliable, and you would never hesitate to have either one "put you to sleep".

However, a puzzling situation developed: somehow and I'll never know how for sure, but a campaign against Dr. Hoagland took place? There were rumors he would ask patients to sign insurance forms in advance of surgery, or that he tried to preach his religious beliefs to individuals during pre anesthetic discussions. Now, Benjie and his wife were strong "born again" type religious people, and they were the same as most folks at that time, wanting to be financially stable. They lived in a big house in Upper Arlington with a swimming pool and beautiful garden, right across the street from Art James, the founder of the James Cancer Hospital at OSU and they were great friends. Further, as I saw it, their aspirations were the same as most doctors, and the same as the prime detractors, whomever they were. There was a rumor about that the board was going to have a meeting with the Administrator to deny Benjie his staff privileges, and I sent out a memo telling them that if I was called to testify, I would proclaim him a great guy, and the most competent anesthesia person ever. There was another rumor that they were objecting to his being a dentist and there was a by-law that only an M.D. could have staff privileges. I pointed out that a dentist, Dr. William Morton, invented and was the first to use ether anesthesia in the year 1819, and that Benjie, in lieu of his years of service to the hospital and patients of Union County, should not be discharged because of such a minor rule infraction, at this late date. Somehow Benjie was gone; he either quit or was discharged but he brought suit against the hospital and received a satisfactory settlement. I helped him get this, when several letters I wrote to his attorneys and the hospital authorities were all in his favor. Meanwhile we had many years of superior anesthesia from Dr. Shelia, and these were her good features, but she lied a little bit about her estimate of Benjies' competence and this was her bad. She ultimately left our hospital after I retired, and I wrote several very positive letters of recommendation for her to work at other institutions.

Physicians And Other Additions To Memorial:

There were about eight or ten practicing doctors on the staff at Memorial when we came in 1953. They all admitted patients for medical therapy, all delivered babies; they took turns on emergency room call and many did minor surgical procedures in their offices like suturing wounds, even casting simple fractures. Surgery was being done on an itinerant basis by doctors coming from adjacent towns and patients were cared for after operations by the local physician. When I arrived, the situation for me was just like an extension of a surgical residency. They gave me a room with a bed and desk, three meals a day, and I lived at the hospital for six weeks while my wife, back in Cleveland, was recuperating from poliomyelitis. The thought that this practice is just like a residency stayed with me for many decades, but there were no interns to do the menial tasks, no visitants to keep happy or impress, just sick patients to care for, with the help and assurance of their private doctor, which was immensely appreciated by me from the outset. I frequently called my trusted buddies at University in Cleveland about advice for tough cases, Jack Cole for one. Also now and then Dr. Maurice Zox, a Columbus physician, who was doing surgery at Memorial for Dr. Walter Burt, would help me with difficult decisions. I was actually taking away part of his livelihood, but he would always say: "Kid, you can do it", when it came to operating on a high-risk patient. His estimation of my upcoming practice was always optimistic and encouraging, and he always called me "kid". Many years later, when I heard that Dr. Zox was retiring I wrote him a letter expressing my thanks for his help and encouragement.

The exact opposite comments were made by Dr. Ed Jenkins and Dr. Bolinger. Dr. Jenkins met me in the hall one day and with a wry smile he said: "Son, I hate to tell you this, but you are going to starve here, there's not enough surgery, I only do one or two cases a week here". A few days later, Dr. Bolinger stopped me in the same hall, took me aside and in a hushed tone said: "Son, you made a bad decision coming here, these doctors will send you patientS and then after six months will demand a fee split". These events occurred some fifty years ago, why do I remember every word from these fine gentlemen? Fortunately for us, none of their predictions came true!

Intellectual Additions:

The first real specialist addition to our staff was in orthopedics, and I don't know how we were so lucky to get Dr. Willis Kubiac. He just happened, no one that I knew solicited him to come, he was on staff at all the Columbus hospitals, Riverside, Mt. Carmel, University, but he liked the country atmosphere at Memorial. He rarely showed up at Saturday morning University rounds with patients, and Dr. Zollinger gave his discussions the "cold shoulder" treatment, in my mind, partly because he had a foreign name, or perhaps because he traveled and operated at numerous hospitals other than University. Willis was a devout intellectual type. When he arrived, in between cases, we could always count on intense discussions with Dr. MacIvor and Dr. Hurl, sometimes with me, about the philosophy of Immanuel Kant, Roger Bacon, Shakespeare, Kipling and others. Once, we discussed the "Four stumbling blocks to wisdom" by Roger Bacon, and I told him that I could never remember the exact words, so he scribbled them out on a piece of scrap paper that I retain to this day: 1) Custom. 2) The perfection of undisciplined senses. 3) The influence of unworthy authority and 4) Concealment of ignorance by the ostentation of seeming wisdom. Every time I view these words that he wrote, it reminds me what a master orthopedic surgeon he was, pin a hip, pound a medullary nail through a broken femur, none that I knew were ever better. However, like all of us, he had a few bad habits that irked the record room folks for one and the nurses for two. Medical records he hated to dictate, and he would accumulate twenty or thirty operations before recording any, with Becky Hilbert, the boss, harassing him all the time, finally getting him to give her something routine to put in the charts. We all knew he could never remember the details of every operation. Number two, he was frequently very late for scheduled procedures at our hospital, usually saying that he had emergencies elsewhere, but we all knew he was visiting his many girl friends, one in Plain City and another in Marysville, while we were all waiting for him to appear. All these things considered made him a great addition to Memorial for some twenty years, by the time he retired, things had changed, we were not getting as much trauma, we acquired two and then four physicians, all doing orthopedic procedures, and I was not as closely associated with them. Two of them, after working together for a few years, developed a legal entanglement of their own; a complex situation that I will never understand; the original partner took on an associate, after awhile the associate wanted out of the partnership to practice by himself, the original doctor brought suit and the final edict was that the associate had to set up his practice at least ten miles from Memorial. So, to our misfortune, he had to move his practice to a near-by town, Bellefontaine. After that, the situation improved when we acquired Dr. Mark Stover and Dr. Baker.

In the few decades after we arrived at Memorial, I never thought about a vacation, but I needed to get away for meetings and Bill Parker, a Michigan trained surgeon living in Delaware, Ohio, came and covered for me. However, in about 1970, Dr. Kubiac met Dr. Jake Elberfeld at

James W. Sampsel

Mt. Carmel Hospital in Columbus, where Jake trained, and he decided to try practicing in Marysville. He took up shop in my office with my blessing, and I thought it would be good to have another general surgeon, perhaps assist with decisions and help in operating. However, Jake was strange from the outset. He was a brilliant fellow, passed his American Board exams with flying colors, but he had lots of outside interests, like motorcycles, strange friends from Australia, taking off on trips frequently for spelunking, which is cave exploring. Now we all have our strange habits, and these traits were acceptable, but they were combined with frequent episodes of his being on emergency call, and no one could find him. Of course, they would always call me, and I would reluctantly come in – and the next morning when we discussed the situation, his reasoning was bizarre and usually irrational like: "Well, Jim, it was MacIvor's patient and he never came in". My response would be "But, Jake, MacIvor is a general practitioner and this was a surgical emergency, you're a surgical doctor". Jake would rarely seek consultation on a tough case, maybe I was too distant, or too eager for him to acquire his own experience but I redid several cases for him. As I look back on these days, I should have faced up to the problems, but I thought there was no obvious solution, and perhaps things would always get better. Jake had a lot of patients that loved him and he did a lot of good work. He had a devastating motorcycle accident, some brain damage was suspected, and after that his practice declined, he took a lot of time off; and was troubled right up to the end.

Most everyone thought we were lucky with the acquisition of Dr. Richard Orahood to practice at Memorial. For me it was a real inspiration to have a fellow with his exemplary training, Columbia Medical School, Wangensteen's School of Surgery Residency, research time in New York, MASH unit in Viet Nam, ending with a practice in Delaware, Ohio, with Dr. Bill Parker. Further, Dick received some of his early enthusiasm for medicine and surgery at Memorial, when as a high school student and all through his college career, he would come and help us with operations. And on every vacation from school, he would hang out at our house, spending days talking research and teaching us modern techniques for things you can't imagine, like how to cook Chinese food, make sourdough bread, basketball and scuba diving. He was a "Jack of all trades", a great running back in high school and college and smart. He was the type of person we were always seeking on the admissions committee at Ohio State Medical School, when most members would criticize me all the time for giving preference to athletes.

Fiberoptic endoscopy was coming on when Dr. Orahood arrived at Memorial and he attended a course in New York, came back with the latest methods for colonoscopy, gastroscopy, and we did some complex surgeries together, mostly my helping him.

We did a Whipple operation or two for pancreatic cancer, and several vascular procedures. However, he seemed not completely happy at Memorial, and after a few years, he surprised and saddened me one day by saying he was leaving his practice here and returning to Delaware. His excuse was about wanting to spend more time with his children, and getting them into the Delaware School system. I was confused, but I resorted to a typical response of mine, which was: "You've got to do what you've got to do". I thought about it then some, but there were possibly other reasons that he didn't want to mention, that occurred to me many times over. First of all, he was never really happy with the general practice doctors that sent us cases, and this attitude prompted a visa-versa situation; they often were unhappy with his point of view, especially when they knew he considered their inputs irrelevant to our surgery. There were a few times when he was on call and Walter Burt or Herman Karrer would call me and see if I would see the patient a day later when it was my day. This put me between a "rock and a hard place", but the alternative was to send the patient to Riverside or University. Both of these doctors, and several others, had a habit of visiting their patients when they were in the hospital, sometimes these were surgical patients, and they would often charge for their visit. Dr. Orahood objected to this policy and so did insurer payers eventually. Patients would frequently pay this fee themselves because they felt good when their long time family doctor told them they were doing O.K. I pointed out to Richard several times, possibly wrongly, but in my mind, patients were not as impressed with surgical expertise as they were with the word, confidence and advice of their long time doctor. If their patient had a surgical problem, he or she would go to Memorial if their doctor indicated they might do well there. I was in a little different situation having worked with these physicians for decades, often getting out of bed many nights over sick people with them – so I thought their role in the patient's welfare was important in our setting, and a small fee for an extra visit was O.K. The thought crossed my mind also that Richard objected to my attitude about right-sided abdominal pain usually being appendicitis, and that he thought I was doing unnecessary surgery, but he never expressed this idea. Many other reasons may have influenced his leaving – we could write a whole book on this subject alone – but enough of this, on to a better subject.

Right about this same time period at Memorial, away from the surgical service, we developed a lot of positive things that need mentioning: Dr. John Evans came out of the Air Force Hospital and came home to begin an internal medical practice with emphasis on cardiology. One general practice doctor wrote John a letter right after he established his practice, telling him that "medicine was well taken care of here", and that perhaps he should just be a "gentleman farmer". John's primary contribution, in my mind, was establishing a coronary care unit that saved a lot of lives about that time. Young men were dying of heart attacks for lack of immediate care, and the cardiac ICU made a definite positive impact on this problem. Not only that, but within six months or so, we were crowding his ICU with surgical patients that eventually even developed into a section for immediate postoperative care. I wonder why we never thought of this before? Previous to the surgical ICU, we just recovered postop patients in their room, a mistake on several occasions.

I remember one such incident where we did a routine hysterectomy on a nice lady and she had an inordinate amount of pain and anxiety after surgery, being recovered in her room, and late afternoon we got an emergency call. She went into respiratory arrest after a dose of Morphine that was ordered for pain. She became comatose. We rushed her back to the operating room, intubated her, Carolyn, John, Dr. Karrer and I stayed with her for two days and nights. She never regained consciousness, autopsy could not determine cause of death, no hemorrhage, no emboli, possible irreversible brain damage, maybe overdose of Morphine in a vein? Allergy? Who knows? Dr. Karrer and I talked to the family; they were forewarned for two days. They said they knew we did everything possible. It was the only immediate post op death that we ever had, and I remember every detail.

We become worthy in changing times:

It was in the late seventies and early eighties that we persuaded several people in multiple departments at the University to send a few of their best individuals to work in clinics at Memorial. I think it was a combination of chance events that was responsible for this endeavor: We were all getting the picture that medicine was getting more complex, and specialists were needed in internal medicine, diabetes, respiratory and cardiac diseases, physiotherapy, and even psychiatry. Oncology, with all its new chemotherapy drugs plus hormonal therapy became a specialty. The general practice doctors were either dying or retiring, and they, for the most part, were happy to refer problem cases to specialists. Also, somehow I think, a change in attitude about medical practice in Marysville occurred: We became worthy! Dr. Malcolm MacIvor and I talked to department heads several times before all at once, someone decided it would not be a burden on the University to have clinics here and one of the first was Cardiology. The hospital board and administration also enhanced these changes; for they all required some sort of financial arrangement.

I was informed one day that Dr. John Prior was coming to head a new department of Respiratory Therapy. John was a famous guy around the University, having been the Dean of the Medical School for many years, always taught the course of physical diagnosis; he wrote a book on this subject that was then important for all students. They named the medical library at OSU after Dr. Prior. So, we were overjoyed to have him head this department, but more importantly he brought Dr. Jerry Dixon as his assistant.

Jerry Dixon was a doctor that you "couldn't believe" randomly arrived at your hospital. He had board certification in internal medicine, respiratory therapy and emergency medicine. I like to think that I had some influence on his staying at Memorial, but I'm sure he saw a situation that would be ideal for his talents. He ran the ICU with an "iron hand", took over tough postop problems, evaluated pre-op high-risk patients, was always present to help with emergencies, worked night and day, early morning rounds, evening rounds, could insert Swan-Ganz catheters, subclavian lines, and of course, respiratory therapy of all types, antibiotics and steroids. He and I would occasionally have arguments over fluid volumes, Lasix administration, or when to do tracheostomy, but he usually won out. Jerry was one of the reasons that I gave some preference to athletes being admitted to OSU Medical School. He was a defensive back at Youngstown State while in college. He went to OSU Medical School and had a lot of his advanced training at Hershey, Pa., part of the Penn State Medical School system. One of his additional duties was to take over the private practice of Dr. Walter Burt, in Milford Center when Dr. Burt retired. We all thought that he was "working too hard", and sure enough, we lost him to a heart attack after one of his tennis matches at Olympia in Columbus. We were all saddened; three or four people arrived to cover his duties, but it was never the same! Respiratory Therapy and Cardiology became permanent specialties at Memorial with great doctors, but it all started with Dr. Prior and Jerry!

The other specialty that came about that time was Physical Therapy. Dr. Ernie Johnson, the instigator and long time head of the department at OSU came to Memorial one day a week and established our department, making Bill Morris the Chief of Physical Therapy operations. This specialty improved the state of our patients that had amputations, improving their problems with prostheses, wound care, fracture rehab., other postop problems, including innovative methods for pain control.

The emergency room of a hospital was always the area where complaints originated being the "frontline" for lots of sick people with troubling problems coming for help. The old routine of rotating general practice doctors for the call there became difficult to manage. One by one these physicians had excuses that took them off the call list, sickness, a few died, and finally one or two individuals contracted with the hospital to take over the emergency room. For me, in the seventies and eighties this was a pleasant change, for frequently I would have to visit the emergency room at 2:00 a.m. to care for a truck driver with a minor headache. Actually, this situation, difficulty manning the emergency service with competent physicians in an ever increasing and complex endeavor, was the beginning of a new specialty, Emergency Medicine. Multiple companies arose that employed numerous physicians, rotating about towns in Central Ohio giving twenty-four hour coverage at most hospitals. It became a board specialty, and training ranged about how to care for a new baby, sew up major lacerations, treat heart failure, handle uncooperative drunks, calm chaos, to call the proper specialist when necessary.

There were so many great doctors in these groups that I never knew them all, but one stands out, Dr. Peter Hoy. I remember him because of an incident one night when he called me to see an overweight elderly man with severe abdominal pain. We gave him a shot of Morphine, pain continued, another lower dose of Morphine precipitated respiratory depression and cyanosis, we reverted to Narcan, a drug that counteracts narcotic depression, and things got better, but we had a few harrowing hours together with this resuscitation, never knowing why the crisis developed.

A crisis for the possibility of shutting down the Obstetric Department at Memorial was averted by Dr. Frank Raymond and his brother Norman in the early eighties. How the administration was lucky enough to get Dr. Raymond and Associates to come here, I'll never know? But for some twenty years a well-rounded department functioned, delivering babies, doing sections, gynecology, innovative fiberoptic techniques, all with minimal complications. They also took time out from a busy schedule to do volunteer medical work in foreign lands. Honduras for one. Frank's family background was physician oriented, father, brothers, and a son on his way in medical school. The contribution of his group to the people of Union county can never be adequately measured.

With Dr. Elberfeld gone, and the volume of surgery ever increasing, the hospital administration and board made efforts to get qualified help for the department. They made financial arrangements with several individuals that never consulted me, and that was O.K., for long ago I gave up being the Chief of the Surgery Service. Dr. John Evans was appointed to a new position in the hospital, an intermediary between medical staff and administration. Things were changing in that more careful scrutiny was being given to each staff application. Support people like assistant administrators, social service directors, financial director, nurse coordinator, several others, all had big and important offices provided, and they all had their secretaries. We were still trying to get another young surgeon to take over the duties at Memorial, and along came Mike Barns.

The story of Dr. Barn's at Memorial is relatively brief, but it gave us many months of frustration, deceit, ostentatious display of normalcy, ending in a still troubled settlement. Mike was finishing his surgical training at Oho State University, and we knew he was interested in practice outside the University, possibly Marysville. He sat beside me in rounds on numerous occasions and expressed a desire to join our community practice. As with the other surgeons coming to Marysville, there was no financial arrangement with me, possibly with the hospital, but my role was to get and help any young qualified person into the important task of country surgery. We had a glowing letter of recommendation from Dr. Larry Carey, then Chief of the department, saying that Mike was a great Resident and would make an ideal addition to our hospital staff. I never talked to Dr. Carey personally about this letter, but in retrospect, my thoughts were: Did he not know about the drug related charges against Mike? Did he dismiss them as false? Or did he just consider them incidental, and think Mike would still make a good practicing surgeon? Incidentally, Dr. John Peter Minton, who seldom saw "eye to eye" with Dr. Carey, told me years later that he knew Mike had drug related problems.

Mike came, was admitted to the staff, practiced for several months, brought his own male assistant to the operating room, and this raised questions with the nurses about their role in his procedures. He never asked one single question about procedure or consultation. Everything went O.K. until one morning a female patient from the Reformatory told a nurse and the nurse told Dr. Evans that she thought her surgeon was on drugs and there was a question about nearly operating on the wrong breast in the O.R? Dr. Evans called me and we confronted Mike in the emergency room where he was on call. He was hostile and said, "You guys think I'm on drugs". Dr. Evans cancelled his privileges and I volunteered to take his call, he left but told us that he was on medicine for a cold. This was a Friday afternoon, and he was scheduled for a Monday morning meeting with staff chiefs and he never showed. We scrambled around for information about how to handle this from the OSMA, and we found out that the protocol was to send these problems to a hospital in Newark, Ohio, for further evaluation. I went out to Mike's apartment, talked with him, urged him to preserve his career and go. He went; the course was to be for five days, but he left the facility on the second day. We got an immediate letter from the doctors at the facility saying that his brief evaluation was positive and that we should cancel his surgical privileges, which we did.

Meanwhile the Memorial hospital lawyers uncovered the facts of a judicial action against Dr. Barns, in the previous year while he was a Resident at OSU on the service at Riverside. He was convicted of writing prescriptions for drugs, sharing them and using them with a local bartender, and the judge ordered him into psychiatric therapy weekly for a year or so. He failed to mention this on his application for staff privileges at Memorial. His lawyers threatened to sue the hospital and us, for canceling his privileges with no absolute (chemical) proof that he was on drugs. In many meetings with lawyers, hospital administration, staff members, Dr. Evans, me, all agreed to terms set out by his lawyers: He would resign if we agreed not to give him a bad reference in the future. Everyone approved of this settlement. To make matters worse, he was being sued by a woman that had pancreatic surgery, and we were in court several times over this as well. I later heard from people at OSU, and I was happy to hear that he developed a successful practice in a southern Ohio town.

So there's the complex story that occupied our lives for many months, fortunately intermingled with the main event of doing our daily tasks as best we could. This depiction is only an outline, never knowing for sure the random events that influenced all the actors.

We continued to look for another fellow to share the surgical duties when Dr. Tim Pelfrey appeared from Cincinnati. A good prediction about his personality was given to me by Dr. Peter Hoy in the emergency room one day when he said: "The new surgeon was through here today, and it looks like he's got his sh—- together." This was an indication that he was surprised to see a surgeon with an ego about like his own. This was in the early 1980's and things were changing for me; innovations were occurring, fiberoptic surgery, primarily for gallbladder disease, but also for appendicitis and hernia repair was being championed. I was getting older, and would find it harder to stand four hours over a case, even if it was just assisting Tim. We did a lot of operations together, and I'm sure he learned many things in his first few years, when I would often see the patients in advance, tell them that we were both going to do the surgery, and calm their fears. In a sense, on a larger scale, it was the same that Dr. Zox and others did for me. However, we did thyroids, colons, hysterectomies, and many more together, helping each other. He introduced staplers for quicker anastomosis, and techniques for fiberoptic cholecystectomies, which I helped him with, but never sought the training to accomplish. I figured wisely that I was too old to begin this new form of surgery.

Meanwhile, many other surgical specialties were appearing all over the hospital: We had many years of expert genitourinary service from Dr. Al Kapcar, a surgeon from Marion, Ohio, but the acquisition of Dr. Mike Conrad and associates to establish a new G.U. service was a plus for the institution. They brought in all the new procedures for dealing with prostate cancer and kidney tumors, as well as treatments for the new fad of male sex problems. Several competent eye specialists came, Dr. Charlotte Agnone, for one, whom I knew as a medical student helping with our surgical research at University. Nose, ear, and throat people were hired, and they began doing thyroids, neck masses, nose and throat surgery, including tonsils. The vascular clinic was now well established with Dr. Smead and Dr. Vacarro running it but taking their patients to University for operations.

Dr. Pelfrey needed another hand on the surgery service when I was looking to retire, and Dr. Brad Bryan decided to "cast his lot" at Memorial. I was particularly impressed with his surgical judgement and operative skills when I helped him on a complex pancreatic case early in his practice days.

So, here we come to the end of this chapter, full of incidents that were important to my mind. There were so many progressive changes occurring within the hospital environment that I was happy to not keep up with them, most were good, some were questionable but necessary. I'll try to list some of them: Hospice facilities for the end of life care, social services for home care and physiotherapy, disease pattern changes, expansion of nursing homes associated with the hospital – all of these helping to reduce hospital census. Physician recruiting, advertising, doctor corporations and their owning facilities, assuming the name of "health care provider", - I guess all necessary?

My retirement party was a blast, funny, I have a hard time remembering the very date. I really didn't want it, but I went along because everybody enjoyed it, and the food was good. Dr. Chris Ellison, the new Chief of Surgery at University spoke and said nice things; I worked with his father on rounds some forty years before. Dr. Evans managed to get a new set of Callaway golf irons for me, and they set up a scholarship fund for students that is still in existence, but not functional. I got the new surgical suite named after me, and a plaque outside the door that probably will be collecting dust in the basement after a few years, and that's the way it should be!

Legal Entanglements

Med school, surgical training and the military do not prepare one for dealing with the type of legal issues that developed in Union County about the time we arrived. Controversies swirling around Memorial Hospital in the first year of its existence were not anticipated. Most of the staff physicians were being threatened with legal action by a series of random events that combined to produce the drama. The adopted rule about practicing surgeons having to be board qualified was a factor, but also a mixed bag of egos, personalities, financial issues, and ostentatious displays of anger all contributed.

Enter Dr. Eddie Jenkins, a certified member of the American Board of Surgery, and belonging to the American College of Surgeons as well, had formed the Jenkins' clinic based in the adjacent town of Delaware. Most of the general practicing doctors in Union County, on the staff of the new Memorial Hospital, joined in this enterprise. It was common practice for the local doctor to admit a patient; Dr. Jenkins, an itinerant surgeon (and this is the catch work frowned on by the College) would come over, operate on the patient, return to Delaware, and leave the post op care to the local doc. The clinic would bill the patient and would send a check or cash to reimburse the local doctor for his services.

But it gets more complex: insinuate Dr. Bollinger, a short, stocky fellow, recently migrated from a remote town, had taken a course in surgery at Ohio State University, and wanted on the staff at Memorial, to do surgery. I had difficulty believing this, but Dr. Paul Zaugg, one of the local practitioners, told me that Dr. Bollinger came into his office one day and said: "Send me your surgery. My lawyer, Harvey Crow and I have cancelled checks to show you were fee splitting with the Jenkins

Clinic, and if I don't get your referrals, you'll be prosecuted." He did the same with the other doctors, so there was a mad scramble to get individual lawyers and a staff lawyer to keep Dr. Bollinger from the staff at Memorial. Actually, the hospital board at Memorial didn't know of his threats concerning the fee splitting, but there were allegations of Dr. Bollinger's incompetence that were forwarded by sources from his last place of practice. The communications between Harvey Crow, Dr. Bollinger's lawyer and some of the counsel for the staff doctors were incredible, lying, cheating, profanity, on both sides. I had never really known a lawyer previously and I had always thought they were honest, trustworthy, righteous individuals, but in view of their tactics during the controversies swirling about Memorial Hospital for years I was happy not to need legal representation in this one. Mr. Harvey Crow was eventually disbarred by virtue of some technicality handed down by a sympathetic judge. Clarence Hoopes, a patriarch of local jurists, hired by the staff on a contingency basis, was a friend of the judge in an adjacent county, and the ruling on Mr. Crow was known in advance of the hearing.

Meanwhile Dr. Bollinger practiced medicine from a big impressive house, with an upstairs ballroom, on West 5th Street in Marysville. He had many faithful patients, and he would frequently send one to the emergency room at Memorial Hospital where he was no longer on the staff. The nurse on duty would call a staff member on call, he would come in, declare the case a non-emergency, but the patient would insist on seeing Dr. Bollinger, who would always appear. Mrs. Helmick, the hospital administrator would then come in, call the County Sheriff, and with his persuasion, plus lots of commotion, everyone would go home. Actually, Dr. Bollinger was initially granted a staff appointment for general practice, but an emergency room incident occurred that was deemed inadequate, and his privileges were removed, prompting his filing suit against the Chief of Staff and the hospital board for redress. This was ultimately dismissed, but the emergency room incidents continued. The final set of several events that brought Dr. Bollinger's quest to an end were: One, an early rule about staff privileges at Memorial being dependent on membership in the Union County Medical Society, and he was dismissed from this organization because he missed too many meetings. And, secondly somehow or someone, perhaps Dr. Stricker or Dr. MacIvor, through their friendship with Dr. Jenkins, arranged for him to get privileges to do surgery in the Delaware Hospital. This seemed to satisfy him, and he stopped his efforts to get on the Memorial Staff. Also, with the disbarment of Harvey Crow, the judge had erased the threat of sanctions on Union County doctors and their chaotic staff meetings came to an end.

However, legal matters moved on to the national stage, with the lawyers delight, when several practicing surgeons in Columbus, Ohio, no longer getting referrals from Union County doctors, and no longer able to split fees themselves, complained to the American College of Surgeons that the Jenkins' Clinic was fee splitting and doing itinerate type surgery. There followed meetings in New York and Chicago with Dr. Jenkins, several local doctors, Dr. MacIvor and Dr. Stricker, plus members of the College Ethics Committee. According to the locals, they were all grilled unjustly with advanced prejudice, but the final edict, in a letter, dismissed Dr. Jenkins from the American College. Now this was bad enough, but the American Board of Surgery also "jumped on the bandwagon" and sent a letter stripping him of his American Board certification. He immediately got his lawyers together, brought suit against the American Board and its then president, Dr. Zollinger, the chief of surgery at Ohio State University. Dr. Jenkins claimed that he had the qualifications, passed the examination, and they had no right to remove his board status. This suit was pending when I came to practice in Union County and you can see why Dr. Zollinger was "luke-warm" on our going there. It sounds "corny" but I never heard the term "fee splitting" 'till we came to Union County.

A strange situation regarding fee for service, and at the same time gave me insight into a different type of doctor-patient relationship was an early incident with Dr. Ev Marsh. I remember my considering Dr. Marsh very old (he was perhaps seventy, approaching eighty). He was thin, wrinkled face, had a fixed stare, an occasional horrendous cough that he seemed not to mind, and was slow moving. A graduate of a two year Ohio Medical College, Dr. Marsh's history (and I want this on the record so it will not be lost forever) included giving drop ether on patient's kitchen tables while travelling surgeons from Columbus came, on the train with their nurses and packs, and they accomplished hysterectomies, cholecystectomies and other procedures. The old doctor was physician, financial advisor, and undertaker-arranger for his patients and their families in remote Union County. I was practicing only a few weeks when he sent a child with severe appendicitis, we were happy to do the operation and post op care. A few days after the boy was discharged, we met in the dressing room; he pulled out his wallet, and wanted to pay me for the surgery. I was confused, but somehow I thought the family should know of my fee. So I awkwardly said that I had to send a bill to them and if they were in need, I would make it small. He said for me to send it and he would talk with them. We did many other cases for Dr. Marsh, always on very sick patients, with no more fee problems. I often thought that this occurrence was actually fee splitting in reverse, and it worked out well for me. No other doctor ever discussed financial matters or fee arrangements with me. Perhaps this was because of their experiences with the Jenkins Clinic? I like to think not!

Dr. Jenkins continued to practice surgery in the Delaware Hospital. I don't know whether his suit against the American Board was settled or dropped. About ten years later, he died with renal failure and hypertension. The Columbus Surgical Society, founded with one of its original doctrines to prevent fee splitting, originated in this environment. When I joined, they sent a special accountant to examine my books. The actions of the committee for the American College were severe on Dr. Jenkins, but I guess there was need to assert their moral standards at the time, all changed now with gate keeping, extensive private clinics, advertising and cosmetics. Implication, of course, was that fee splitting by physicians, fostered unnecessary surgery. The local doctors claimed this was not the case, and that the itinerate aspect, with Dr. Jenkins living only twenty miles from Memorial, was not a problem. Compare this with the present, where most specialists live in distant cities, or usually are very far from academic hospitals.

Nevertheless, all these entanglements made it difficult for Memorial to attain status around the University, and we did not become worthy for many years. You might say the bad were obvious, but the good resulted in a now productive Columbus Surgical Society.

The American Board Of Surgery And The American College Of Surgeons

Every medical student with aspirations to become a surgeon had one eye on the American Board qualifications, but one does not really get serious about them until well into training. Late in med school and into surgical internship, you have other concerns, for instance, grades, military duty, finances, or even romances occupying your mind.

The board in general surgery was established in about 1937 and its mission was to create order out of chaos, and to improve surgical care for patients. There were many doctors operating in county and other hospitals, without the five years of approved training or without passing the exams necessary for certification to become a so-called diplomat. This was a common situation in the 1950's, but for me, when we came to Union County, it was serious business; because the Hospital Board, on the recommendations of Dr. MacIvor and others, had voted-in the edict of allowing only board qualified individuals to practice surgery there. Looking back, I am sure my mind had no idea that this was the case when we decided to practice in Union County, but by chance, it turned out to be an advantage for us.

The American Board exams are offered to those with training in selected institutions and we took part one as a written test during our last year of residency at Western Reserve University Hospital. It consisted of some essay portions, asking for discussions of surgical judgements on presented cases, there were segments with multiple choice selection, the combinations covering anatomy, physiology, chemistry, metabolism, mostly science related to surgery at the time. The exam took up a whole day, and weeks later we opened letters, with considerable apprehension, but I received a passing grade, which qualified one to request the second portion.

Part two, the second portion of the examination was a different format, an all day affair, sometimes two days, conducted at various academic centers throughout the country and given about two times each year. I assisted with one of these exams at Ohio State University as a member of the clinical faculty. The format was all oral, two or three examiners in a room, pointed questions, and sometimes observing operations in progress, more questions and comments. A session with surgical pathology specimens of the day, more questions about technique, observing x-rays and other tests with more discussion were also included.

The usual procedure was for people to request part two after they had been out of a formal training program or into practice for a year or two, and that's what I did. The exam was offered in Cincinnati, a drive-to city for us, so after a year in practice, I decided to take it there. I remember calling mentors and friends from my training in Cleveland, and inquiring about the exam and its format. Did I need to study? I talked with Jack Cole, who later became the chief of surgery at Yale, and his words were: "Sammy, don't worry, you'll know everything they'll ask you". This made me feel good; because I was extra busy with practice and had little time for study. However, Jack was wrong: They hit me with a lot of cardiac physiology, pressure values in various heart chambers, chemistry of gallstone formation, and a lot of other stuff that I guess made my answers vague. My letter came a few weeks later and, of course, they stated that my effort was notable, but I had failed, and for me to repeat the exam at my convenience in a year or two. Only at this writing, do I entertain the remote thought that somehow my grades on this exam were influenced by the legal entanglements at Memorial. At the time, absolutely, it never entered my mind, but in retrospect, considering the initial attitude of the American College toward me, it was a remote possibility. Contrary to this idea was the fact that my own impression was of my poor performance, and that the other individuals from Ohio State faculty, one a vascular surgeon and another, Bob Watson a Markel Scholar; also failed the examination.

So, in a few months, I began plans for a second shot at the board exam. This time, it was to be given at Duke University, in Durham, North Carolina. We consulted Dr. Zollinger, he offered a few suggestions, and he was confident we could pass it with study. I took on one afternoon a week helping to teach surgery in the anatomy lab at OSU. We obtained the names of surgery department heads about the country that were board examiners and I sent my secretary to the library to get a list and a copy of all the papers they wrote in the last ten years. Dr. Zollinger wrote us a letter to the chief surgeon at Duke University requesting he allow us to attend their rounds and conferences. We went down there a week in advance, met people, got a feel for their research and major activities. At that time, would you believe, they were doing extensive sympathectomies for hypertension. We stayed in a local motel, studied the college manual on surgical diseases every night. It all paid off; they asked me about the sympathetic nervous system and hypertension, I couldn't wait to answer. I remember discussing the anatomy of hiatus hernia as if I invented it. Another portion was in the OR where the topic of colon cancer surgery came up. We had read Dr. Turnbull's papers, and the examiner gave me the impression that he was learning. But despite all our preparation, the biggest break for me was a random event when a fellow came out of his exam, told me they asked him about a kidney specimen with Wilms' tumors. The examiner showed me the same kidney tumor and I had to act as if I was thinking for a while before I answered all I knew about Wilms' tumor. Of course, we all passed the exam and the letter came in a month or so with a certificate to hang on our office wall. I found out later that all the ladies back in Memorial Hospital Record Room, led by one Belle Orahood, were praying for me to pass the exam, and there was no way I would fail with that kind of help.

The American College of Surgeons is an educational association created in 1913 to improve the quality of care for patients. The usual procedure is to apply for membership after one was qualified and passed the American Board, submit cases from your practice or teaching activities, come for an interview with three members of the society, and await becoming a member, or a "fellow", thus allowing you to place FACS after your name and to hang your certificate on the wall. However my quest for membership took unusual and understandable turns because of the legal entanglements in Union County. I had passed the Board exams, enmassed all my case reports from a year in practice, and went for my interview in Cincinnati, where three fellows gave me a "going over". I remember their saying: "Why doctor, your records show you did one major case a day in your first years of practice, how is that possible?" Of course, they were implying how could this be possible without fee splitting. They even asked me if I knew Dr. Jenkins and what I thought about him! Needless to say,

James W. Sampsel

I received a letter from the College, informing me to submit cases again in the future and my application was turned down.

I rushed to the University to see Dr. Zollinger, a recent high official in the College, and he said perhaps he could help. In a few weeks he called me in and asked if I would submit to a fellow from Chicago coming to Union county and Memorial, visiting and examining. I was overjoyed. He came, stayed in a local motel, went in to our operating rooms and clinics. I turned him over to my secretary to examine books and office records daily. He returned to Chicago after a week at Memorial. About a month later, a letter came informing me that I had been granted a fellowship in the society, this followed by a certificate for me to hand on my office wall. These prizes were accompanied by a set of regulations that we all had to adhere to as fellows; most I was already practicing, including no advertising. One interesting regulation, which I have frequently storied to young surgeons, was that we were not allowed to put our name with bold type in the phone book. It was OK to put FACS after our name, but no dark, bold type. How far is this from the mind set from medicinal and physician advertising today?

The complex and extensive educational and other precepts of the American College, everyone should agree, are reasons why American Surgery now leads the world, all good, hardly any bad.

Nurses

At an emotionally filled service for one of our young nurses, Donna Wickline, I had a prepared comment to deliver if called on by the Reverend, but never got to express it: that, "If there is a heaven, nurses should walk right in when they die, young or old, good or bad". Two or three had actually died during my tenure, some unexpectedly, and I'm sure they all will be up there doing their virtuous work. It would be a continuation of their life activities in hospitals, operating rooms, wards, clinics, doctors offices, wherein they spend decades making contributions after young and eager years in preparation. Their ventures often have them plodding dark halls of hospitals at night, odd hours, frequently on call, sometimes emptying bedpans, responding to the requires of sick people in distress.

One could liken nurses' actions to reconnaissance squadrons in the military, out front, probing, and making initial contact with sick people and anxious relatives. What's more, accommodating to the wrath of some doctors was routine, even when finding themselves caught between the conflicts of doctors and administrators. On a nearer equal level with the thoughts of patients, nurse's opinions were salient features for relieving anxiety, creating placidity, and acquiring confidence in the population for the hospital and doctors. Nowhere are these characteristics more evident than in a small community institution like Memorial, or as essential for assisting a country surgical practice.

On the page margins, I have listed the names of many of the nurses that dedicated a great part of their lives to the tasks of that time and place. For the most part they were "home grown", raised and living in the county. Untold numbers of stories existed for each individual mentioned in the list. But my recollections are those related to the surgical services and here, there are what I consider interesting, sometimes comical, but hopefully realistic anecdotes relating to nurses' activities and connected events.

Nurses:

Kim Andrews
Barbara Barr
Glena Beams
Janet Berry
Dorothy Bowersmith
Marilyn Botkins
Barbara Bowman
Jan Bright
Marge Brown
Martha Bulan
Barbara Bushong
Elaine Cox
Mary Jane Crothers
Madeline Fuson
Liz Griffith
Mary Gruenbaum
Karen Hall
Frances Helmick
Gladys Hesson
Linda Howell
Janice Humble
Shelby Jackson
Beth Johnson
Helen Kaiser
Marsha Kiss

Mary Kleiber
Jo Knight
Andy Mayer
Karen Masters
Flora Meddles
Carolyn Mitchell
Linda Nelson
Mary Newman
Mary Ann Norris
Dorothy Painter
Doris Pfarr
Norma Riggs
Wiladine Rausch
Diane Salyers
Anna Shoemaker
Nadia Shuran
Polly Stevens
Betty Symbolik
Bonnie Thorpe
Ruth Ann Tiller
Marsha Todd
Carolyn Trees
Madge Troesch
Donna Wickline

Narratives:

How could anyone disagree with the concept of randomness when we, just by a series of circumstances acquired a surgical nurse like Jan Bright? As a graduate of the Mt. Carmel School of Nursing, she had perfection as a primary attribute, sometimes to excess. Through the years, in all sorts of trying situations, she served as first assistant, handling the instrument tables, knowing what you wanted before you did, even giving opinions about surgical judgements when asked. In operating rooms like ours, probably the same throughout the world, we all saw intense times mixed with a few relaxed moments. Everyone's mindset was concentrated on the extreme situation most of the time, stopping massive bleeding from fragmented spleens, torn vena cavae, securing delicate anastomoses of bile ducts, ureters or arteries, to name a few. But when the stressful part of the operation was over, tension relieved, routine wound closure often was accompanied by light conversation. Anesthetists, circulating nurses, assistants, even support people outside the room, all usually entered these discussions. Bright, Benjie Hoagland, at the head of the table, and I would combine opinions in these memorable exchanges of views.

As an example: We often talked about relativity and the Universe, especially when Einstein's formula $E=Mc^2$ was popular. If only we could exceed the speed of light? We bantered Jan with: "There was a girl named Bright, who moved beyond the speed of light. She went away one day, in a relative way, and returned the previous night." On the subject of food and restaurants, we formulated the general postulate: "The dimmer the lights, the higher the price". One morning after a stressful case, we learned about the Gulf of Tonkin and the Vietnam War. Dr.Linscott, helping that morning, was in favor, I was against, lots of banter, none of it mattered but many had sons ultimately serving there.

Strangely, the most consistent cliché in our Operating room, and in all the others I've ever been in, was: during closure, the conversation would turn to sex. These diversions were not malicious or licentious, usually comical or remotely suggestive like: What did you think of the beauty pageant on TV last night? Or a clean joke with a punch line of "everybody's got to be someplace" the irrelevant response of the wife's lover, hiding in the closet naked, when husband returns to get his brief case unexpectedly, opens the closet door and says: "What are you doing in there?" and the lover says something like: "Well, everybody's got to be someplace."

No-Bed Brown

In the mid-sixties, when our hospital had seventy-five beds, always full, Marge Brown, a young and energetic nurse, with the help of Miss Madeline Fuson her supervisor, and Mrs. Helmick, the administrator, was more or less the admission officer. They conjured up a system of categories for admissions: emergencies, semi-emergencies, and electives. Every doctor especially the busy ones, Burt, MacIvor, Karrer, Zaugg, Stricker, always considered every patient an emergency. And, of course, I was always calling her with surgical problems high on the list – Marge's response was always the same: "No beds today until someone is discharged". She caught flack from everyone, but managed to "weather the storm" with beds in the halls, even next to the nurse's station. The Fire Department complained – These were stressful times. I gave her the name "No bed" and it stuck.

The Winter Of '78

Several days in the winter of '78 set a record for snowfall, and would you believe, one of our more ambitious girls, Andy Mayer, whose first name is really Dorma Lee, drove right into it. Andy was another Mt. Carmel graduate, could not stand imperfection, often loud, said "gosh" a lot. She lived in Plain City with family and husband Burl, one of the premier farmers of the area. One night we were working late, she embarked from the hospital at about 2:00 a.m. It was raining hard. The rain turned to snow, the temperature dropped, snow came down for two days straight; she did not make it home, and was reported missing. Dr. Kukla and I on skies, traveled the road to Plain City the next day looking for her car. Actually her car was stopped on the road by wind and snow, covered, about a mile from her home. She thought about getting out and walking but could not open the doors. The temperature dropped to around zero, she moved from front to back seats in the car, curling up and covering with an old sheet. Icicles formed on the car ceiling. After about seventeen hours of internment, she was found when a neighbor, going to town on a snowmobile, spotted the antenna of her car sticking out of a big snowdrift. Only Andy could have survived this ordeal, and we were lucky to still have a great surgical nurse.

Candy Stripe Program Pays Off:

In the early days of the hospital, someone started a volunteer program for schoolgirls, whereby they periodically came to Memorial and did minor tasks. They had striped pink uniforms, all very cute. I remember Barbara Bowman as one of these, and she returned to ultimately be the O. R. supervisor for many years. She handled the egos of surgeons, anesthesia people, and other nurses, with a disregarding aplomb. Every doctor wanted the 8 o'clock schedule, anesthesia was always late, tonsils always had to be done, dire emergencies occurred almost daily; there were problems fitting them all in!

She had an energetic supporting cast: My vision is of Helen Kaiser, a nurse from Plain City, devoted, slightly obese, scurrying about, striving to please everyone, while trying to disregard and mask her increasing multiple sclerosis that was producing pain and weakness. And there was Wiladine Rausch, a helper from obstetrics, on her hands and knees, cleaning up blood from the floor around the operating table so that we could start another waiting emergency.

Stories surround the role of Mary Kleiber, stool donor, and author of multiple euphemisms in the department scene. Mary worked for her Nurses' Aide degree later in her life, perhaps at 40 or so. She was a young beauty queen, raised a family, a "down to earth type lady". "Hurray, hurray, the first of May, outdoor screwing begins today" was one of her axioms that we remember to say each year while she was about, and long after she retired. The other noteworthy event involving Mary, somewhat comical but actually made contribution, was her acquiescing to become the donor for fecal bacteriotherapy. This was a reported form of treatment for a serious disease called pseudomembranous colitis that arose in the 60's and 70's, and when cephalosporins and other antibiotics changed intestinal flora to allow the overgrowth of clostridium difficile, the causative organism. A few surgical patients developed this severe, sometimes life threatening diarrhea that we treated with enemas of diluted stool from the healthy donor, Mary. A funny side issue with this affair occurred when I mentioned our method of treatment to Al Kapcar, our G.U. consultant, a comical guy. He reeled back against the wall in amazement and said; "Well, at least it's cheap!"

Another nurse that became a surgical supervisor was Karen Hall, whom I called "little Mother", because she was small and a mother. Like others, she was devoted, and one late afternoon into the night, we had a case together, still on my conscience. It illustrates how things can look very bad, but rarely by some miracle turn out good. It was some poor old lady with intestinal obstruction and with more adhesions than you could ever imagine. Somehow, we were into the case with Karen assisting and only a circulator plus an anesthetist in the room. The operation went on for hours; we were all tired, there was disrupted and adhesed bowel, we had to repair perhaps five or six tears. We finally gave up and I said to "Little Mother" with lots of emotion, that I was sure this nice lady would die. I can still see it like a bad dream sequence –Karen reacting frightened but saddened. Surprise – the patient recovered and lived.

Floor Nurses And The Clinics:

The outpatient hospital clinics at Memorial were established as an innovation to accommodate specialization. After a time, I began to see most of my postoperative patients, have consultations, and do minor operations there. The nurses in the clinic were all helpful and supportive, many assisting with procedures ranging from being present at pelvic exams to complex grafts, flaps, caring for central lines, filling chromofusor pumps to name-drop a few of their tasks. Many nurses working on floor units were also later assigned clinic jobs.

One of these nurses, with duty on floor units, when she was young and eager, Mary Jane Crothers, struggled with me over a poor unfortunate patient, and I still remember his name, John Sasser. It was when we did minor operations in floor rooms; John had major multiple mets from colon cancer and a retracting sigmoid colostomy. We exerted our efforts with local anesthesia, to get the mucosa above skin surface as part of the palliative therapy.

Years later, when M. J., was working as a clinic nurse, her "claim to fame" in my mind was when she "stormed out of the room", throwing down instruments, no longer tolerating the fault finding criticism of Dr. Orahood. "Dickie" had this bizarre idea that to get maximum performance from folks, adverse criticism was important. He used it to extreme here, and was finally challenged by a nurse. Another incident in the clinic with Mary Jane, that I sort of regret to mention, was when the girls made a cake with candles for me on my birthday. I informed everyone in advance that I would not appear for this celebration. They went ahead with it; I faked an emergency and did not show up. "There was no joy in Mudville" for weeks.

One of the sad events in the Clinic was when Donna Wickline passed away with ovarian cancer. Donna assisted on many operations and she would hum popular tunes softly, while we were working. I even requested a few, urging her to lean toward the classics. Her renditions would get really intense as the operation got more complicated, like when our split graft looked too small to cover a defect, or we had trouble stopping some small bleeder!

Barbara Bushong was one of the pioneer nurses that took advanced training in Oncology when it became a specialty. She was quietly devoted to patients, gave completely of herself to working in the clinic for years. Her role was helping with operations, scheduling, reassuring folks getting chemotherapy treatments. She knew about all the drugs, always up for the latest information, a prime example of why people came to Memorial for their cancer therapy.

Another girl with empathy and understanding for the difficult patient was Betty Symbolik. She was a quiet, subjective type, ever helpful. I challenged her one morning with my memory lapse: We saw some poor, unfortunately unhappy lady with breast cancer complaining about something. In the room, we advised a chest film and CAT scan. We came out to the desk and Betty said: "Aren't you going to order the tests?" I said: "What tests?" My mind was a complete blank. I could not remember the patient, the tests, or anything about the morning. Betty was alarmed and concerned; she called Dr. Dixon, our medical consultant. He eventually diagnosed "brain overload" from my having had a day- before research trip to NIH. Everyone was happy that the lapse was temporary.

The Obstetrical Department was possibly the most important component of the hospital – Dr. MacIvor and I saved it from extinction when there was talk of closing it. There was a host of nurses and aides that made it function and a few characters stick in my mind: One was the nurse supervisor that started her journey there on opening day, and remained for many decades. Mary Ann Norris was outgoing, confident, knew more about deliveries than most doctors, trained as an Army nurse in W.W.II, She ran the department with assertive efficiency, sometimes even criticizing doctors and often improvising in the early days. Mary Ann's attitude spilled over to everyone working with the mothers, babies and she made it always a joy and pleasure to visit there. Another nurse in Obstetrics, with the exact opposite personality to Mary Ann's was Martha Bulin, an apparent maiden lady, quiet, had a wry smile accompanying opinions, and lived alone in a secluded house across the street from the hospital. She was obsessively religious, reminded one of a nun, now and then hinting to convert folks to her beliefs, but devoted to pregnant ladies and their babies; an example of two entirely different functioning styles making momentous contributions.

The untold stories of nurse activities could be endless. We have portrayed only a few that have occurred during a given time and place. A blur in my memory is of nursing in later years with increasing complex demands, male intrusions, specialization, accompanied by comings and goings. When the final chapter is written for each individual nurse, yes, they should walk right into heaven.

My Uncle Charlie, Other Doctors And Events Of Influence!

Individual associations influence each other's thoughts and actions, many significantly, like the ingredients of chemical or biological reactions; the interplay of personalities were paramount in the lives of all country surgeons. There were so many in this category for me that defining them is difficult; limiting them to physicians makes it easier. No Nobel Prize winners here, just ordinary people doing their everyday thing, frequently not realizing, but sometimes intentionally creating deliberate events that markedly influenced others, for good or for bad. Many of these events occurred before productive years, some during. But most were by individuals of the greatest generation, as described by Tom Brokaw[1] in his book, all products of a different time and place.

Can you believe that a college student would come home on vacation, and before going out on a date, would drop off his chubby, kid nephew at the local drug store soda fountain for a cherry ice cream delight? When "Hippie" as we called him, would come home, the word would be out, and I would run down the mountain to bother him and his buddies, as we all went to the local garbage dump to shoot rats with his .22 rifle. Another example illustrating our relationship was his response to a stupid childhood incident of sleepwalking. When he was home, I always came to my grandmother's house, a small row type in the coal town, with a cramped winding staircase to a third floor with two rooms, unbearably hot in the summer time. It was a chore to get down to the one bathroom, and one night sleep walking, I peed in his bedroom slippers, which were

---

1   The greatest generation, Tom Brokaw (1998)

beside his bed in the adjacent third floor room. Instead of beating me up, he thought it was strange and funny, laughed all the way to the bathroom to clean them.

This upstairs bedroom was the same where I first began to read a set of books called The Hahnemann Monthly, depicting case reports from the Hahnemann Hospital in Philadelphia. They were all lined up on a shelf in the cramped bed room, and I would leaf through them sometimes looking for nude pictures, hardly understanding any of the writing, but knowing they were related to doctoring.

Uncle Charlie's career progressed through college, med school, training at Philadelphia General Hospital, into practice at Bristol, Pennsylvania in Buck's County, all carefully monitored by me. There were many times when I was in high school, while he was an extern at the local hospital that he arranged for me to observe operations and visit. But the random salient event occurred in 1939, when he called on the phone, a few days after my graduation from high school and said: "You get your ass to the post office and request an application to this year's class at Penn State. I'll get you the money." I was excited to hear this and I sent it in. My dad had just given me a shirt for a graduation present, and told me that he could not send me to college because we had other family members also in need. Working, playing ball, hanging out with buddies occupied the time of a naïve seventeen-year-old, with no thoughts given to world events like World War II brewing. It took adult advice to know starting into education was critical. Charlie helped with encouragement and finances all during my college days, and his advice was a deciding factor for my going to a Cleveland Medical School.

Charlie was drafted and went to the service with compelled eagerness, but sad leaving his wife and newborn son. He was assigned to the 37th Division as a Captain in a medical battalion, and I remember visiting at Indian Town Gap, a staging area, before the outfit left for the South Pacific. He and his buddies got a big laugh over the ASTP patch on my uniform, indicating the Army Student Training Program. They all said it reminded them of a "flaming bed pan". There was all haw-hawing but a sense of their being happy that I was in med school, not going with them right now. They all joked about being back home and returning to practice in six months or so, and so did we.

The unit served on Guadalcanal and Bouganville before transfer to the 10th Army on Okinawa. He died there along with lots of his buddies in a Japanese air raid, on day ten of the campaign. He is buried in Hawaii, and one of our nurses visited there, photographed his grave for me. These events are part of the reasons why I have always had difficulty relaxing or having fun, as my daughter was always after me to learn, even in old age. Somehow, the dilemma in my deep conscious mind may be, why our lives continued while others were terminated? I have been enamored with the words of Simon Wiesenthal, a Holocaust survivor, and applied to this county surgeon in many ways: "Survival is a privilege which entails obligation".

Herman Karrer, M.D.

When we first came to Union County, I went to see Dr. Karrer, a prominent member of the Staff at Memorial, and a busy practitioner in Plain City, a nearby town with a large Amish community. My impressions of him on that day, all good, were eventually borne out, as we ultimately enmassed many days and nights together, working on untold numbers of surgical problems. Herman was a solid, courageous, respecting, forthright individual. He was the house calling, sitting beside the bed, caring doctor's-doctor, always eager to be proper, taking courses, learning to read EKG's – yet he was the first to seek consultation for his patients. He and his nurse-wife Margaret were highly religious, Presbyterian, and many of his patients were ministers. He had this solid view of life; because, as a doctor, he had been on the beach at Normandy, day five of the invasion, all across France and Germany with Patton's 3rd army, and in his mind, anything after that was a bonus. When in the hospital, he was frequently the first to answer emergency calls, to the ER or rooms, even in the days when doctors were getting sued for connections with emergencies. When his patient's were being operated upon, he was an excellent assistant, always staying to the end of the procedure so he could talk with the relatives about the outcome. This made him frequently angry if his cases were delayed, justifiably so, much to my chagrin. The Ohio State Medical Association rated him "The Physician of the Year" one time, but I have always been thankful that random events led me to work, for many decades with great men like Herman Karrer.

Malcolm Macivor, M.D.

Malcolm was a guy that you immediately liked. He was an organizer, would enter a room with flamboyance, clicking of heels, and the suggestion of a Scottish army Major, right down to the small mustache, never in doubt. He had his office for general practice in a small house, right near the center of town, where his father before him had an established practice, in past time when a house call might take days to accomplish, and there were about five doctors in Union County with no hospital. Malcolm interned at St. Luke's Hospital in Cleveland and brought to Memorial many by-laws of that institution, including one restricting surgical practice to trained physicians. His early training was deep into the humanities because he was initially interested in the ministry. This explained why he could come up with a poem or a literary passage for any situation, and frequently would expound while assisting at surgery. We learned more about Kipling, Byron, Shelly, and Shakespeare that was ever encountered by the team in school. One of his favorite old Navy terms, that he acquired as a doctor on a carrier off the coast of Korea was: "Stand by for a ram". He would exclaim this if we were encountering a tough situation during an operation or if he had bad news to tell me about some patient! He dealt with a lot of bad news as Coroner of Union County for about thirty years; always handled it with aplomb and dignity. When he entered the room on a house call, things were immediately better – made more so there, and in his office by a shot of Vitamin B12.

His practice was widespread throughout the county. He knew everything about everybody, who was sleeping with whom, who was related to whom, what was the price of wool? for he kept sheep on his land and would help shear them periodically.

Witticisms were his "stock in trade" and many were comical but profound: "Are you re-inventing the wheel down there?" "Learning more and more about less and less" – several favorite statements of his when I would return from research at the University. He never wanted to retire; because, he thought: "When you retire you become a non-entity". On going to Florida:

"It is God's waiting room" or "The land of the living dead". His was a confounding habit of latinizing phrases and terms, hard to remember, but for instance: "inflagrante delicto" for a situation where one of our doctors was alleged to have had sex with a nurse, being discovered in the hospital library by an aide. "Bubus Americanus" was his definition of the crowds of people at University and other football games, for he was anti-athletics of any kind. And, when I would tell him about the virtues of skiing or hitting a tennis ball, he would respond by accusing me of looking for the "excelsior orgasmo". Civil war history was high on his agenda and frequently his vacations were spent visiting and studying battlefields like

The Wilderness, Bull Run, and Gettysburg. An avid gardener, he and a friend, Marvin Twig, PhD Botanist, (would you believe this small, quiet, gentle fellow, with a name like Marvin Twig, a friend of us all, was a PhD with expertise in caring for trees and shrubs) would travel to Maryland State Forests to study trees and plants.

Malcolm's wife, Barbara, was a graduate nurse from the prestigious Francis Payne Bolton School in Cleveland. She developed breast cancer, we treated her and she was on Tamoxifen, an estrogen blocker, for seven or eight years, before we knew that switching to an aromatase inhibitor, whose function was to prevent estrogen formation, was the best therapy. A tumor developed in the opposite breast with sudden generalized spread and demise. Malcolm had a lot of support from his family and office personnel, but some time later, after a session with friends, on philosophy and Scotch Whiskey, he went to bed, and was found not alive in the morning. We were all saddened, but everyone agreed it was a great way to go. He never had to retire and be a non-entity.

H.E. Stricker, M.D.

H.E. Stricker was a maverick type general practice doctor, a University of Michigan graduate, delivered many hundreds of babies, and during our time was the physician at the Ohio Reformatory for Women. He was the exact opposite of Dr. Karrer and Dr. MacIvor, in that he had a disdain for medical meetings or anything connected to University teaching, as I wrote in a poem about him, he constantly objected to rules and regulations. One had the impression that his insight was not always up to standards, but any deficiency was overshadowed by his intense concern for his patients. This was especially true in the OB and GYN fields where, as I look back and reflect, my thoughts are that he was really way ahead of his time: objecting to silly rules we had for tubal ligations, hysterectomies, and sections, he was always pushing for me to do operations that would be done routinely now, but then were withheld probably to patient's disadvantage. We were trying hard and ultimately succeeded in overcoming being publicly dubbed "uterus-less Union County".

"Strick" was an internationally known wireless radio operator, with sources originating from his home on the then outskirts of town. Wireless radio was way ahead of the computer Internet in providing worldwide communication. One time, he made contact with stations in Thailand and Viet Nam, tried to get our son on the line but failed.

The bad about H. E. was minimal: now and then he would disappear on a weekend, allegedly gambling and drinking with his cohorts, and other doctors would have to cover for him, but this was rare. Late in his career, one day, he had a fatal heart attack while on a visit to a nearby town. It was rumored that a nurse at the Reformatory "bugged him so" that it contributed to his demise, and I believe this to be true.

Walter Burt, M.D.

In the days when the 75-bed Memorial Hospital was filled to capacity, Walter Burt had more patients admitted than any other doctor. He saw some 48-50 patients per day in his office at Milford Center, a close-by farming and railroad town in Union County. It was the first time I ever heard of folks, in a doctor's office, taking a numbered ticket off a spindle to be seen sequentially. He was a smart guy, an Edward G. Robinson (a then popular movie actor) look-alike, a graduate cum-laude from Northwestern University Medical School, and how he ended up in Milford Center, I'll never know. Quiet and unassuming in most medical meetings, he rarely objected to policies, and he was not included in the legal battles about the hospital because in the first year of Memorial, his surgical consultant was Dr. Zox, a Columbus surgeon. Walter was also a prominent entrepreneur, in that he had interests in local meatpacking, and he owned the first public laundry establishment, coin operated, that anyone ever heard of. Despite his wealth, his demeanor was always modest, and with his retirement, he took up volunteer doctoring on Indian Reservations in Western U.S.A. No patient ever had a bad word to say about Walter, and I guess his influence on me was his confidence, and the constant stream of surgical patients that we handled together.

Maurice Zox, M.D.

Maury was on the staff at Memorial, doing surgery for Walter Burt and a few other doctors. When I came, he helped and encouraged me in many ways. First of all he said: "Call me, kid, if you need help", and I did. Never mind that I was taking away part of his livelihood, but when he helped with a few difficult cases, he insisted that I dictate as the surgeon and send my proper fee. This was in the first year or two of our time at Memorial, and not only did I learn a lot from him, but he introduced my wife and me to his family at several gatherings, and had us to dinner at his Columbus Club. It was at one of these affairs that we encountered one of his wife's interesting relatives, a survivor from a Nazi death camp, proudly showing the numbers tattooed on her arm. Maury was Jewish, married into a prominent Columbus family, and I think this may have been one of the reasons his request for a faculty position at the University was refused. This bothered him deeply and I knew that Dr. Zollinger, the Chief then, had certain prejudices. The bad about Maury was that he was loud, and husbands of nurses objected to his ever friendly attitude. But for me, the good was his encouraging and assisting demeanor to a "kid" country surgeon, with absolutely nothing for him to gain by it. All this is gone from everyone's mind now, save mine, and his only thanks was in a letter I wrote to him when his retirement was announced.

Bernard Ingmire, M.D.

Bernie was another general practice physician in Plain City, the near-by town that had Dr. Karrer and an Osteopathic physician, Dr. Adams, the latter person always completely ignored by the M. D.'s. Dr. Ingmire was secondary to Dr. Karrer in the number of patients they had, but he had a more liberal attitude, smoked cigarettes, would take on individuals with alcohol and other addictions that other doctors turned away. We had many complex cases together, including the young boy with a rare muscle tumor of the rib cage in which we ended up treating with radioactive ribbons inserted by a specialist trained at Memorial Hospital in New York.

While working over some poor sick patient with Bernie, I would get his philosophy on many subjects, but one I remember was his impression that described the three primary functions of a physician: to relieve pain, minister to anxiety and to save lives. For some reason, he thought the last was questionable? His own life's final event was with lung cancer. I visited with him several times in his plain house on a busy street, when he was sick. We watched "The Rifleman" on TV together, his favorite program. He was calm and affable right up to the end.

Paul Zaugg, M.D.

Paulie was at Memorial Hospital from its beginning and he was in the thick of legal issues threatening the doctors in the first few years. His wife, Mae, was our trusted anesthesiologist. Their relationship was compatible, but became strange in later years, perhaps being related in some way to the chance occurrence of their daughter Cindy, being born with cerebral palsy. She was a joy to them, but at the same time a burden, for their lives centered about her care and providing for her future. Paul's practice was extensive and his patients loved him. He lived and worked in a huge, old, three-storied house on a prominent corner of town where he had his office in one portion. A large part of his work was with hospital patients, which made for our treating a variety of cases together. One I remember was removing a femoral artery thrombosis with the innovative Fogarty balloon catheter. Surgical assistance was one of Paulie's main attributes because he liked it and extra training in surgery at OSU Med School was his choice. A secondary demanding venture was his interest in antique dealing, whereby he traveled around the country, and outside as well, obtaining desks, lamps, old chairs, which he displayed and sold from a historical old house, thought to have had a connection with slave freedom, located on a side street near the center of town. His on and off companion in this business was an interior decorator of local fame. Some years later, Paulie developed a series of strange diseases, one in which we did a major operation. After arriving at a diagnosis, we contacted a friend from my Army days, then on the staff at Memorial in New York, and Paulie went there for a more radical procedure and chemotherapy. He surmounted all these difficulties with aplomb and retired with family to Florida, the so-called "land of the living dead". Years later, we learned of his demise through a Memorial Service for him at his local church.

Fred Callaway, M.D.

You arrive in a place like Union County and there are people who just happen to be there before you; they influence you with their presence, combined with thoughts you have about them, initially, and as time goes on. Fred was about seventy years old when we arrived; deludedly we considered him an old-old man. He was a graduate of some eccentric medical school, but a wise general practitioner, read the New England Journal regularly, did tonsillectomies and set fractures with drop ether anesthetics in his small office before the hospital was established, plus continuing these procedures at Memorial, with few or no complications, and he was the first Chief of Staff.

There was talk of Fred's being distantly related to Daniel Boone. His near constant chew of tobacco and his love for coon hunting made one think that this myth might not be an exaggeration. Several times, in the first few years, I tromped through the woods at night with Fred, dogs and his buddies, seeking the vicious raccoon. I could never share their thrill of shining a light into that creatures eyes and blasting it out of a tree. The dogs, some three hundred dollars apiece, were shared with his friend,

Bill Coleman, who ultimately became the Chairman of the Democratic Committee that helped elect John F. Kennedy. We collected the dogs from their enclosure at Coleman's and hiked to the nearest woods, four or five strong; a moonlit night, cool and crisp was preferred. The camaraderie and exercise were pluses, but an army after one little critter?

The distant connection to Daniel Boone was probably not responsible for Fred's being a ladies man. There were many stories to substantiate this claim, like the one where some female patient asked what she should do about her husband wanting sex everyday? His response: "Get down on your knees and thank heaven". A personal note, further attesting to this assertion was, when we had a party at our house, serving Fish House Punch, the Old Coot comically backed my young wife into a closet where she had to object to his advances!

Fred's wife Ethel was an interesting character, a do-gooder, made ham and egg breakfast for me at their Frank Lloyd Wright House, after my first night in Marysville. She was one of those old ladies, always with a fixed purpose, somewhat spacey. She told a local policeman once: "You should be out chasing criminals" when he stopped her for speeding. Another time, she came out to inspect our house in the country that we were renting, walked in, unknown to my wife, inspected the whole place, said "This will do nicely". Dolly wondered who was this old lady? But she was acting as the wife of the Chief of Staff, wanting to help the new young doctor and his family. Ethel was the one that had her common bile duct full of stones, which we were fortunate to relieve, but later in life she developed pancreatic cancer. We discovered after abdominal exploration that it was inoperable. A delegation of her relatives came from the East, demanded another opinion. We sent her to Dr. John Peter Minton at the University; he re-explored her only to arrive at the same conclusion.

Fred's practice gradually declined as he restricted it to doing tonsil operations at Memorial. He became ill from what we thought was "old age", retired, and passed away quietly with no fan fare.

John Linscott M.D.
Rodney Hurl, M.D.

There were, of course, many other physicians of influence, like the later arriving general practice doctors, Jack Linscott and Rodney Hurl. Both developed large followings – Over fifteen or twenty years, each with their unique styles.

Jack was a World War II infantry veteran and was a teacher before going to OSU Medical School. His manner was often subjective, never abrasive, always laughed along with you. We had many cases together but one patient to remember was Ellen Saam and her husband. Ellen had unrelenting abdominal pain despite all our efforts to requite it. It was in the old days before pain was a much-needed medical specialty, and surgical intervention was not the answer for her. Years went by, and every month or so, she would come in, beautifully dressed and tell me: "If you had my pain, you'd do something about it". Her husband would frequently be waiting for me as I made early morning rounds, to request pain medication, which Dr. Linscott and I would order sparingly because of State Medical Board mandates, always a dilemma!

Dr. Hurl was different, a graduate of Temple Medical School in Philadelphia, Pa; he had military duty in the Air Force. A lot of his time and energies were spent volunteering on the Board of his small college, Bethany, in West Virginia, where he also had many famous relatives, connected to the now extinct steel industry and he would describe their antics in detail, repeatedly. These descriptions were sometimes combined with political declarations, always conservative, always anti-JKF. You might say Rod could be intrusive, or excessively opinionated, but he had an uncanny knack for understanding and directing financial matters that were prime movers in forming a corporation that provided office space for decades and ended up making us money!

This came about through an interesting set of chance negative relationships that developed between Rodney and the then President of the Hospital Board, P.C. Williams. For some obscure reason, unknown to me for sure, Rod and P.C. never saw "eye to eye" on any subject. Perhaps it started right after Rod and Dr. Linscott appeared on the scene. P.C. gave a party-reception for doctors and other personnel at his impressive town home and forgot to invite Rodney. Who knows whether he really forgot? But in any case, I think this may have been a starting point for Dr. Hurl being anti-hospital and anti-administration.

Actually, Rod made an initial effort to engage Memorial Hospital in a scheme that would have had benefit for all. I remember going with him to see P.C., board president and Rod suggested that the field adjacent to the hospital would be an ideal area to build a facility housing doctor's offices, and that it could be accomplished with physician-hospital cooperation. For some reason the proposition was "turned down". So Rod sought another local entrepreneur, Ezra Stocksdale, who jumped at the chance to form a corporation with a group of doctors, completely separated from the hospital. I became part of this group; however, my input to the corporation was like one "floating down the Colorado River on a raft"; building cost per square foot, rents, bank loans, mortgages, bonuses, being all foreign to me, but all handled adroitly by Rodney. As time went on, my greatest pleasure with the group was the camaraderie encountered in the twice yearly meeting and knowing that I "need not to worry" about all those details.

The following are physicians that remain on my mind; they resided outside of Union County. Three of them of world renown, and one from a small Pa. Hospital that no one, but a few remember.

Robert Zollinger, M.D.

My relationships with Dr. Robert Zollinger, brief as they were, and usually at a distance, proved to be among the most productive of my career; although initially strange, and made awesome by his eloquent position in the world of surgery and academics. Trained at Massachusetts General Hospital in Boston, home of Elliot Cutler, Harvard's Harvey Cushing, in a direct line with William Halstead, all the God's of Surgery were in his camp. He and his associate Eddie Ellison were then in charge of this big surgery service at Ohio State University, and I was elated when they added my name to the faculty as a lowly clinical instructor. Dr. Zollinger often had a comic approach, mentioning at one of my early brief visits, "Did I miss the expensive carpet that Bill Holden had in his fancy office at Western Reserve?" The "Big Z" always wore monogrammed shirts, had manicured fingernails, and a tremendous ego tunnel, but how else could you head a world-renowned surgery service? In the operating room he was a superb anatomist, but sometimes his antics were mixed comic and realistic, like when he would make residents or nurses "go stand in the corner" for some minor mistake or hesitation. No one ever talked back to him, but occasionally someone would leave in despair. His hallmarks in conferences and especially in the famous Saturday morning Rounds were protocol and simplicity. Several times, he would demand medical students leave the room if they were not properly dressed with shirt and tie. Slide presentations of pictures and diagrams of complex topics were made simple so that the least of us could decipher. One point that I remember was when he flashed a slide of my fellow resident, Bill Drucker, who later became Chief at the University of Virginia, showing fructose metabolism that was so complicated that, he pointed out, "No one would even try to understand it".

A Nobel Prize never materialized for Dr. Zollinger, but it probably should have. One of the main contributions of his, along with his associate, Dr. Ellison, was the original concept that a tumor, a new growth, in a given organ, the pancreas, for instance, could exert an influence on other structures by producing hormones or other molecules, to cause harm. This revelation spawned other research with eventual clinical benefit in ulcer disease and tumor pathology. Dr. Z's imprint on surgery was also enhanced by political accomplishments within the American Board and the American College of Surgeons, his being elected to the highest office in both of these institutions. He retired and took quarters in the John Pryor Medical Library at OSU to work on his memoirs, and I visited with him many times there. His style was the same, comic-assertive, admonishing me not to do fatty operations, and predicting no good for OSU surgery with a newly appointed female at the helm.

Arthur James, M.D.

When one sees the multi-storied cancer hospital at OSU, with recent plans for enlargement, and thinks about the thousands treated each month there, few remember the trials and tribulations of Art James when he began to develop this institution. It took years from inception to fruition for this dream. The untold numbers of ranking PhD. researchers and modern sought-after clinicians working there now, hardly ever nor could they think about the initial frustrations of this guy. Art was the exact opposite of what you imagined a prominent surgeon to be. He was quiet, unassuming, spoke in soft tones, hardly ever comical or assertive, always helpful. Foremost, he was trained as a specialized cancer surgeon at Memorial in New York, and he came to the faculty at OSU at a time when there was some disdain regarding the practicality of the speciality. Somewhat the same attitude was prominent for years as he labored to fund and produce the cancer hospital that bears his name. Initially, all the directors of medical institutions in the city of Columbus, along with many at his own University were skeptical of the need for a cancer hospital. How he persevered and brought together all the participants we'll never know.

Life's random, paradoxical events were nowhere more operative than here: as the James Cancer Hospital flourished, Art gradually deteriorated with Alzheimer's dementia. He retired to his home in Upper Arlington and became completely dependent on his great wife, Millie, with the help of a devoted nurse, in constant attendance.

Mention needs to be made of two more individuals, one from the research field, and another from the formative years who provided influences that come to mind: Dr. Cecille Leucthenberger was in charge of the research group in Pathology at Western Reserve and she was kind enough to "take me in" for six months or so. Their primary mission in this laboratory was identifying and measuring DNA in cell nuclei, about the same time that James Watson and Frances Crick were describing the structure of this molecule as a double helix. Cecille was a German lady, fled from the Nazis to the Karolinska Institute in Sweden, where she worked with Caspersson measuring nucleic acids by light absorption techniques. She was taking a chance on this surgeon coming into her research group, tolerating his initial ineptness and gradually introducing him to the workings of her staff in the laboratory, and the complex nature of the techniques. I learned about emotions there, not quite as intense as in surgery, a different level but constant devotion to the work, writing, always examining, meetings, discussions, often personal, rarely with families included in the gatherings.

William Leach, M.D.

Dr. William Leach was the head surgeon at Locust Mountain State Hospital, of my hometown in Pennsylvania. His quiet and unassuming ways were a major influence along with initial exposures to his performance in the operating room there. I would get a friendly enthusiastic greeting, when returning on vacations from college, always invited to lunch with the group where they discussed cases and topics of the day. Dr. Leach was confident, caring, but forceful and in a quiet, unassuming way subtly influenced a scared, interested kid into thinking about some day becoming a doctor-surgeon, just like he was.

Case Reports With
Human Interest:

Case reports of patients are no longer accepted for publication in most scientific journals, there being no market for individual successes or failures, save in the New England Journal of Medicine where they combine a single case each week with high-powered opinions and multiple modern tests to arrive at a diagnosis. They make each instance liken to a computer game, where you can entertain your own diagnosis with a preliminary gathering of facts, get the complex data as you progress, and finally arrive at some far out opinion with the experts. Modern editors, like those of Surgery, Oncology, Nature Medicine and many others, are enamored with the German Thru Put concept (see Research Chapter) that demands thousands of data points or cases before reporting.

I hope you will find the unique human interest aspects of the events in this chapter, most good, some bad, not worldly momentous but for individuals involved, their anxieties, struggles, hope, triumphs, tragedies, most chance encounters, interesting parts of the human condition and prominent features of a country surgery practice.

A Missed Passenger On Christmas Eve:

First is the story of Waldemere Krudle. The night was wintry, 10-15 degrees, wind and blowing snow on the road between Marysville and Milford Center. The squad was called out for an accident about 10 o'clock, and they brought in two young men with various injuries, cuts and a few fractures. After they were admitted and comfortable, they inquired about their fellow passengers, and they asked how Wally was doing. We said

"Who's Wally?" They said "There were three of us in the car." We called the squad and told them there was a missed person out there, it was well after midnight, and they went to the scene of the accident. They found Wally behind a big snowbank away from the roadside, face down, unconscious, with hands and arms extended.

His fingers and toes were frozen and exam signs made us suspect intracranial bleeding. With the help of Chris Theodotou, our Consultant Neurosurgeon, we explored the skull and evacuated a large hematoma; also requiring a second evacuation several days later. Post op, he was placed in a room with the windows wide open to maintain hypothermia, which at the time was in vogue for brain injured and other severe trauma cases. He remained non-responsive and after a few days another complication developed, breathing problems that required a respirator, then, we used the type for polio patients called the "iron lung", body and chest enclosed in a barrel-like housing, tight seal at the neck with head exposed. He remained in this state for weeks but his respiratory status improved somewhat. I remember the difficulty we had and the valiant effort of the nurses, with intravenous fluids and input-output monitoring while he was in the respirator.

We learned that he was a mechanical engineering student at Case University in Cleveland, and his parents were engineering people, emigrated from Poland, living in Dayton. The parents stayed at our hospital and a local motel. The were deeply religious, went to mass every day, prayed for his recovery. We all thought this was a nice effort, but would prove to be of no avail. However, one day, about 6 weeks after the accident, he responded to his mother's daily greeting by opening his eyes, and from then on, it was all improvement. After some eight weeks with us, they took him to a Dayton hospital for rehabilitation and he responded well.

His father, whose name also was Wally, was immensely appreciative of our efforts, would call me and visit the hospital from time to time, informing us of his progress. One day in the early Fall, I was on the golf course and someone came out and told me Wally Krudle was at the hospital and wanted to see me. I thought, "Damn, this old guy comes at an inopportune time", but I reluctantly came in because I always had other chores at the hospital. When I arrived, they directed me to the dining room, and I get tears in my eyes every time I tell this story: There, sitting in a wheel chair, surrounded by nurses and other hospital people was young Waldemere Krudle, smiling, holding out his hand to greet me. He had signs of residual but improving brain damage and several amputated fingers. We talked. He was planning on going back to Case University in a year. I later learned that he was the top student in his class before the accident and years later he graduated in the top ten.

I know there are many scientific studies surrounding the merit of prayer in relation to its value in seriously injured patients, some positive, most negative, but this was an outstanding single incident in my mind. Perhaps the salient chance factor here was the initial hypothermia provided by the cold night and the snow beside the road.

A Will To Survive:
The number two story is that
of Emma Canivito:

This saga could only be acted out in a county setting where all the actors were real examples of bizarre human relationships, prison protocol, religion, surgery and unusual survival. Emma was serving a life sentence at the Ohio Reformatory for Woman. She had been the notorious poison queen of Cleveland, alleged to have done in about ten people, while working for the mafia. In prison she was the pet of Ma Riley, the Warden, who provided her with her own cozy cell, having access to an adjacent lovely garden and walkway, plus individual meals and entertainment. Emma was sixty-eight years old, massively obese, weighed about 280 pounds, was five foot three, being treated by Dr. Sticker for diabetes and hypertension.

Her journey into surgery began, when she developed abdominal pain, signs of definite peritoneal irritation, we thought might be appendicitis. Our surgical team was mobilized, nurses, anesthesia, packs and we headed to the prison operating room. When her abdomen was explored, we found a small portion of small bowel, the mid ileum, was gangrenous with a localized mesenteric thrombosis, probably venous. The area was resected, bowel hooked-up, abdomen closed, and she did fine for about forty-eight hours. We gave her the whole gamut of treatment, fluids, heparin, antibiotics, diabetic control, but on the second afternoon she developed shock, more pain, bloody diarrhea, and we knew she had extension of her thrombotic disease, a common sequel of mesenteric thrombosis. She was transported to Memorial for another operative exploration.

Here's where the human interest component begins: Outside the open doors of our operating room during the procedure, gathered Ma Riley, my wife Dolly, Father Falvey, the local Catholic priest, and several selected women prisoners that were friends. I'll never forget Ma's touching assurance as Emma was wheeled by: "Don't worry, Emma, Mother is here praying for you." They all stayed until the end of the procedure, all happy when Emma was wheeled out still alive. Father Falvey was an old Irishman from Boston, devoted to saving souls at the prison, and believe me, this took a lot of saving. My wife Dolly was one of his parishioners that he frequently called for transportation; because he was not able to drive. She picked him up at the rectory, took him to the hospital, and stayed 'til he was ready to return. Ma Riley was brought to the hospital by daughter Jean, who also stayed.

The surgery was extensive, the entire small bowel was gangrenous, save for about fifteen centimeters proximal, beyond the Ligament of Treitz, and the blood supply was intact to the right colon and the cecum, with a stub of ileum preserving the ileo-cecal valve. We removed all the gangrenous stuff, anastomosed, ligated vessels, washed things out, closed wounds, and thought it would be only "a matter of time" with Emma, for nobody lived with about 90% small bowel removed. However, she had a strange, calm postoperative course, returned to the prison in ten days and got great care there. Six months later, she was still having six to ten bowel movements per day, her weight dropped from 285 down to 110 pounds, her diabetes and hypertension disappeared.

We wrote a paper about this case that was published in the Ohio State Medical Journal in 1959. About the same time people were getting interested in operations for massive life threatening obesity, even some considering small bowel bypass. Dr. Stricker's name was on the publication and even though he was always against meetings and medical journals, for years, he had a copy of this journal proudly displayed on a table in his living room. Further, at that time, we were studying functional hyperplasia that occurred in remaining organs after partial removals, like in liver, kidney, and even small bowel (see research chapter).

Emma died of heart failure some ten years later, and damn, I was away at a meeting and never got an autopsy, which I was ready to do myself if necessary. We could have had a real break-through studying her liver and changes in her small bowel. We had x-rays and functional studies that contributed a lot to solving the problems – so you might say again: everything can have its bad and good, she came to prison for killing people, but she contributed to the overall good eventually. End of story!

A Damn Good Fellow:

The number three tale is about Max Raney, my insurance agent, introduced to me by Dr. Sticker when we first arrived in town. The surgical interest in this case, not exactly minimal, is overshadowed by Max's personality, and how you all might know someone with this unique habit as an old man, to interject swear words into every expression he uttered. As a young man, he was part of a group that burned a cross on the lawn of John Evans. Old John, as we knew him, loved by all, was the great, great grandchild of a slave that acquired considerable land in Union County after the Civil War. John was then a prominent farmer, whose wife Helen was a member of the then Governor Rhode's Cabinet and whose son, young John became a staff member at Memorial in internal medicine. Max was John's insurance agent, and remained so even after the cross burning incident – John knew that Max was part of the group, but they were still friends?

The medical excursion began for Max when he was on a fishing trip in far off Canada with some of his buddies, and he developed abdominal pain. They put him in a car, drove about twelve hours, arrived at the hospital with him in dire distress. He had a ruptured gallbladder with bile and inflammation all over the peritoneum. We washed out the cavity, removed the offending organ, and closed a big wound that later had abscess and partial separation. This complication was what kept his coming back to the clinic for repeated visits, each one getting more and more comical as time went on. For instance: We would say "Well Max, how's it going today?" And he would answer "O.K. Doc, but I feel like I just fell out of a God damn hearse". About that time I had a son that was the same age and a friend of one of his nephews. He told me: "These God damn boys are really nice Son's of bitchin kids, Doc". There was a funeral for one of his friends that he attended at the Catholic church and his expression about the sermon was: "Jesus Christ Doc, Father Falvey gave John a God damn great send off to wherever in the Hell he's going." These are only a few of Max's favorites that he batted out in a constant low monotone. Eventually age took its toll with some memory loss, and I had to switch insurance agents, because he lost some money for us. He developed a neoplastic condition that was just being described, a precursor of multiple myeloma, elevated specific IgG in his serum, followed by extensive bone destruction that did not respond to therapy.

The Bishop's Renunciation

The main comical and human interest aspect of this narrative would never happen in the present day, for it was a decade when hospital beds were at a premium in the Columbus area, filled to capacity, and we always had trouble getting permission to transfer high risk patients from someone, sometimes only some resident on call.

This night, a bunch of high ranking Methodist Bishops were on their way to some religious meeting in Columbus. Their lead car had a major accident on Route #31, where a tree covered cross road was often the source of trauma for us, but this time the squad brought two overweight Bishops and their wives to our emergency room. There was chaos, phone calls, clergy from their entourage milling around, two were seriously injured probably from sitting in front seats, and their wives from back seats had only cuts and bruises. We employed the usual emergency trauma postulates, airway establishment, central lines with fluid administration, evaluation with blood work and x-rays. The number one Bishop had an immediate respiratory problem due to multiple rib fractures; the anterior chest cavity was sort of detached, and could not expand properly. He went right away to our intensive care unit where we applied upward traction to his sternum with tongs, pulleys over the bed connected to weights by ropes, an idea we got from some trauma journal that improved his breathing to a stable state.

We had the number two Bishop in bad shape with free air in the abdomen, so we thought it a good idea to transfer the number one stable Bishop to the thoracic service at Riverside Methodist Hospital in Columbus. Dr. Malcolm MacIvor, an avowed Presbyterian, was the local doctor on emergency call that night, always looking and acting like a British Army Major, said "We'll call Riverside Methodist and get him transferred". He called, told them we had this Methodist Bishop that needed immediate thoracic care – but the person at their emergency room said: "Sorry, we have no beds available." Malcolm said: "What!!! This patient is the main Bishop of the whole Eastern United States and needs immediate care." Believe it or not the response was the same, "No beds." So Malcolm got really "ticked off", called Mount Carmel, a Catholic Hospital, and they said straight away: "Send the Bishop right down". We did and he went to surgery, had chest stabilization, and a great recovery.

Is this an instance of chance factors influencing human behavior or what? I wonder what the administrators at Riverside thought when they read the papers about the accident?

The number two Bishop, we took to surgery the same night, completed a complex situation that we'll cover in the trauma chapter, was transferred to Riverside with courteous aplomb about four days later.

The Truck Drivers Lament:

This is another tale about clergy being injured, but not as seriously, and the intriguing parts of the story are the enhancing players, all brought together by a single chance occurrence. It starts in the very center of our small town, the county seat of Union County. Father Falvey, the local parish priest, standing on the pavement at Main and Center streets, and a trailer tractor truck came around the corner, the back wheels came up over the curb and went over Father's foot. Now, of course, he collapsed at the scene and was brought to our emergency room by the squad. Meanwhile, the truck driver was informed of the accident; he was a religious Italian fellow from New York, came to the hospital to pay his respects to the injured. When he found out the identity of the victim, he exclaimed, "Oh, my God, I've run over a priest", promptly fainted and had to be resuscitated. With help of the nurses, he eventually recovered and went on his way.

But for Father Falvey it was the beginning of months of pain and trouble; the injury would have been devastating to a young healthy individual, but Father was old, obese and not a good candidate for healing. Multiple fractures and soft tissue injury took their toll, long term daily dressing, antibiotics, and débridements were necessary. The bishop sent a young priest to take over the parish duties.

Enter Father Jim Ogurchock, a scholar, a teacher, schooled in the philosophy of Kant and Bacon, he impressed Dr. MacIvor, a Presbyterian, our local philosophical expert, with numerous discussions, yet the young priest took right up with the duties of daily dressing and caring for Father's nasty wound, in more than true christian fashion, putting up with daily admonitions about his inadequacies. What's more, Father Jim had to put up with Aunt Julie's cooking, she being the aged aunt of Father Falvey, his housekeeper and cook. Father Jim had to teach her to make toasted cheeses sandwiches on Fridays, to put the cheese and bread together before toasting. Malcolm MacIvor and I visited the rectory many times before things returned to normal. Father Ogurchock became a life-long friend. So, in this case, good things resulted from a disconnected bad initiation.

The Indavertently Bad Is Always Out There:

As a country surgeon, you wake up every morning trying to do the right thing, and in thousands of instances what you think is the right thing turns out for the good, but the bad is always out there, haunting your memory, depressing you for months, or years sometimes, and in your mind you re-live those events, even long after you retire. The following cases are examples of the bad from my mind. There may be more that I've suppressed, some appear in other chapters. I guess you could say they all are of intense human interest for me.

Surrepticious Ovarian Cancer:

I was in practice about ten years when a young woman came in to Dr. H.E. Stricker's office, and wanted her ovaries removed. Her mother lived in another town, had just died with ovarian cancer. He called and said "Jim, this lady wants an operation to remove her ovaries. She's worried because her mother had this cancer." He was really serious about this, as he was with all his patients, but he frequently over-reacted and would often send me patients that didn't really need surgery, so I didn't really want to see this lady, but I said, "H.E., we can't just do that, but send her over and I'll talk to her". Her examination was entirely normal; we talked and she was still insistent; so I said let's get another opinion. I sent her to see Dr. Rich Fulton, a medical consultant from Columbus, who came to our hospital occasionally. He called me and said "Jim, this lady wants an operation, so at least take a look for her". We did, and of course everything, including the ovaries was absolutely normal. There was no way I was going to deprive this young woman of her estrogen on a whim, not to mention the criticism from the pathologist for removing normal tissue and doing unnecessary surgery. She was happy after the exploration and her fears were abated.

Some five years later, she went to another doctor with complaints of abdominal fullness and pain. He sent her for consultation and I remember seeing her in the emergency room; she had a fixed mass palpated on pelvic exam. It was ovarian cancer, and she died with it in about six months. She or her relatives never thought to blame me for this disaster. Later on in my tenure, right before I retired, when molecular genetic studies became practical, and finding mutations in BRCA-1 or BRCA-2 genes pointed out increased risk for breast or ovarian cancers, removing normal tissue was often indicated. I guess you could say for this lady, at a given time and place, we did the wrong thing for the right reason? All by chance? The good thing about this case is that here after I always leaned toward removing ovaries if Mothers had ovarian cancer, especially if BCR2 genes are mutated.

A Test Ordered But Not Waited For:

Somehow, for some forty years of surgical practice, I avoided being sued for so called "wrongful death" of a patient. Even though you have to be schooled to overcome the loss of life or the agony of a patient that cannot be relieved the loss and complication is especially difficult to bear for patient's family and surgeon, when it is unexpected. In this particular case, increasing liver failure was completely unforeseen, went on for months, became irreversible and ended in the demise of this nice lady. She died after months of treatment at the liver specialty service of University Hospital, and the autopsy showed massive centrilobular liver necrosis, the cause never determined for sure, but at that time Halothane hepatitis was suspected and other similar case reports appearing in the late 1980s indicted this anesthetic, so that it was deemed not safe for adult use.

My part in this story began when Dr. MacIvor asked me to see this lady in the hospital with upper abdominal pain, tenderness, and tests indicating gallbladder disease. We advised operation, but she improved in the hospital, and we discussed her going home for awhile, but she wanted it done then. This was on a Friday afternoon, and among the many tests we ordered, one was a hepatitis screen. On Monday morning, we did her operation without incident, but I was confused and worried when immediately after the procedure a nurse came in and showed me her positive Hepatitis B antibody level. That night she had an inordinate amount of pain and the next day she became jaundiced, confused, and had a high temperature. I thought perhaps we had injured her common bile duct or missed a stone blocking it. The next day jaundice increased and her liver function studies were all markedly elevated. We arranged for her transfer to the University for further study and care. We scrambled around to find the latest studies about hepatitis screens, and I felt a little better when I discovered that the positive antibody meant that she was probably immune to hepatitis B, while the B antigen test being negative meant no active disease at the time of our operation. However, the rub for me and the thing that has plagued my conscience for years is that had I waited to see the hepatitis report with the positive antibody, I would have delayed or cancelled her operation on that day. Never mind that this positive test probably had nothing to do with her demise, and that the real culprit was the Halothane toxicity in an obese lady. The other significant random event for this patient was that our anesthesiologist was new to our institution, had come from training where Halothane use was strongly advocated, while our other specialists did not use this product.

About a year and ten months after these episodes, not completely surprising to me, one morning, on my way to the hospital, a gentleman approached, asked my name, handed me a subpoena, just like given to any other criminal, murderer, rapist or bank robber. There followed numerous depositions with my own insurance lawyers, and the opposition's. The latter, a nurse-lawyer constantly wanted me to admit that my decision to operate on this woman caused her demise and she was correct, but she didn't know Halothane toxicity was the cause. They kept saying the problem was hepatitis B, and their so-called experts really never knew that the positive antibody was in our favor. My own blood test was positive for Hepatitis B antibody. Nevertheless, we ultimately settled the case for a million dollars from my medical insurance; the anesthesia doctor's insurance did the same. My wife wanted me to fight it, take it to a jury locally, but I thought it would go on for years, and a local judge, whom we had previously operated on, advised that we settle. There is no way the months of anxiety and grief for this patient, her family, and me can be erased. Time has not done it!

Not Cognizant Of Inordinate Pain:

Another case that has plagued my mind on the bad side, one I have often had to shut out of my active memory years after it developed, not at Memorial, but in the military, a young Spanish soldier with a cavalry recon. outfit fell off a half track and fractured his mid tibia. It was at Losey Field in South Western Puerto Rico. He was brought in, given drop ether anesthesia, and with some manipulation the fracture lined up nicely. I was young; somewhere recently I had read about tight plaster to hold fracture position, and I applied it with little padding. The final x-ray showed perfect alignment, and that evening everyone retired feeling good about the result. The boy had tremendous pain all night, and in the morning another x-ray showed the fracture had displaced again, so I sent him on to the General Hospital in San Juan. Several months later, a surgeon from the General Hospital called to remind me that the boy required weeks of valiant effort to save his leg. Skin necrosis over the fracture site had occurred, converting it into a compound situation and they were still using flaps and grafts to get healing. I still think about the boy's pain, that night, when I should have loosened the cast, forgetting about the fracture position. Ever since that day, I always overused padding beneath casts, and I became a skeptic about new opinions in medical journals. Here again, I guess you could say I did the wrong thing for the right reason.

Criminal Slight Of Hand, Justified?

In the form of a confession for forgiveness I advance the next tale of human interest, call it what you will, good or bad, but all turned out well. I was away at a meeting, and a serious accident occurred, the patient came to Memorial, Dr. Zox was covering for me, Dr. Zaugg was on call at the emergency room. The middle aged man had serious abdominal injuries, including a ruptured spleen. They operated on him and everything went well. I returned from the meeting three days later and the patient was recovering, but he developed fever, tenderness, and we suspected an abscess was developing. Abdominal x-rays showed a strange situation: Two radiopaque tape markers in the upper abdomen. We removed the abdominal dressing, repeated the x-rays; the same situation obtained. The patient continued to have fever, pain, tenderness. We advised re-exploration. Liz Griffith was the OR nurse that evening, and I remember removing two surgical tapes from the instrument table, after the count, when she went out of the room to get instruments. I dropped the tapes under the table.

We explored the abdomen. There was some serous reaction around the tapes; they were mixed with tapes from the table, everything else was normal, we washed out the abdomen, the secondary closure went well. The tape count at the end of the procedure was normal. After everyone went home, I retrieved the tapes from under the table and discarded them. Dr. Zaugg helped with both operations, and he agreed to what I was doing. He had special rapport with this family, and I think it would have been O.K. with them if we had informed them about the tapes but we never did. I never knew if Liz Griffith, the Chief O.R. nurse on call that night knew of this underhanded maneuver, or not, but I never asked. Our routine was always to have two people count tapes before and after every case. To my knowledge, we had never lost a tape or an instrument in any other patient at Memorial. I never informed Dr. Zox about this incident.

Let's Not Forget:

Every doctor should, or probably has been in the role of patient's relative, waiting for word after operations, visiting daily, looking for progress, fearing sudden calls at night, worrying about outcomes, when you know lots of the possible bad details. As time goes by in the hospital, and you've given up hope of getting out in a few days, the value of aides and nurses, doing everyday tasks, like those associated with bed and bathroom, not complicated, but for the patient the most important.

A case in point was my wife Dolly, who had most of her large intestine resected for diverticulitis by Dr. Pelfrey and his friend Sal , the latter a very competent surgeon from Cincinnati, who came to Memorial especially to do my wife's operation. We thought she'd be in the hospital for a week or ten days, but it turned into six weeks or so with multiple complications, and I was caring for her many of these trying weeks, because Dr. Pelfrey informed us before surgery that he was leaving on vacation, and we thought we'd be home by then, but not so. She had pain, pain, pain, and her gastric suction tube kept pulling out large quantities of fluid, never abating, requiring intensive IV therapy to keep up. I asked Dr. Orahood to come over from Delaware to restart her subclavian line. Meanwhile, she developed a left femoral vein thrombosis, heparin had to be given daily, and it was back to ICU several times. Still her GI tract did not open up and we considered taking her back to O.R. fearing obstruction. In retrospect, the best idea for the cause of the adynamic bowel was a side effect of her pain medication, but who knows for sure? There were times during these weeks when Dr. MacIvor and I thought of giving up on her because of so much pain and desperate suffering, but she persevered, improved by increments day by day, made so by the aides coming in every morning, changing the sheets, making the bed, and giving the daily greeting: "Let's get out of bed and walk today". These jovial, well intended directions were more helpful than any medicine, required no fancy training, no qualifying exams, just a bright personality every day, cheerful, even though her own life was full of setbacks and disappointments.

In this final paragraph, I will outline a few incidents that are still in my mind, but lots of the details have faded. One afternoon we stopped hemorrhage from a uterine artery that bled after a ligature, applied by a visiting gynecologist during a hysterectomy, came off. Then, there was the interesting story of the man on vacation in Greece, developed abdominal pain, was hospitalized, needed an operation, got on a plane, came back to Memorial and we resected a small segment of obstructed small intestine. A nurse recently reminded me of the pregnant lady who got kicked by her cow and suffered a ruptured spleen. We had an elderly Scotch lady with cancer of the pancreas, we resected, and every year she would want to make "one more" trip back to Scotland. After four or five years of this, we thought her desire to return was a deciding factor in her survival; we were about to report the case, dug out the old pathology slides, but decided the original diagnosis was wrong, it was all bizarre pancreatitis.

I was recently reminded to include the story of Roger Morley, a young, strong individual, a privilege to know, let alone care for. Working as a lineman for the D. P. & L. (Dayton Power and Light Co.) on a pole twenty or thirty feet in the air, he suddenly touched a high-tension wire and was thrown to the ground. How survival of the electrical aspect or the fall came about, we'll never know?

In the emergency room, he was in shock and had a huge burn over the scapula and one on his foot. The back lesion had destroyed skin and muscle required months of debridement, flaps and grafts. He was ever grateful, and gave us credit for saving his life – but not so- he saved his own life with his will to survive and his acceptance of long term pain and suffering.

There are so many other human interest stories (cases) from one small hospital; some appearing in different chapters. No fiction here, all examples of human minds and actions caught up in chance occurrences.

Innovations And Inventions During Our Time:

While American medicine was helping to transfer the World Center of Science and Industry from Europe to the United States, there were many innovations that made their mark on our patient care. Perhaps not always world shaking, nor spectacular, but at the time and place, essential when added to the work of country surgery.

Antibiotic Therapy:

High on the list was the introduction of antibiotic therapy. World War II figured in its development, but one must say work of Pasteur, Semuelweiss, Lister, and others laid the groundwork in decades gone by. But the discovery of penicillin mold as an anti-bacterial by Alexander Fleming, his initial struggles and later efforts to translate the discoveries into clinical usefulness are legendary. Actually, who was to know that penicillin was going to be the landmark for the multiple groups that followed? The tetracyclines, aminoglycosides, to name a few from the ensuing billion-dollar industry that developed.

We used all the groups through the years, especially as resistance developed to a given type. About all our abdominal and trauma procedures were accompanied by antibiotics during and later as prophylaxis. The extensive industry that developed was a far cry from my initial experience as a student at Reserve, when there was a rumor that some patient survived an infection in a, mid-sagittal sinus (an intracranial fatal disease) after receiving this new drug called penicillin.

Another antibacterial molecule developed even before penicillin, not as heralded, but I first saw it as a powder, called Prontosil, to place on wounds. Dr. Leach at Locust Mountain Hospital had a smile on his face as he showed me how it helped to heal infected wounds. It was a sulfa molecule, and its early introduction by the Germans was a spin off of their dye industry. All the antibacterial drugs had mostly good, but some ultimate undue features, as extensive applications developed toxic situations, like allergies, bacterial resistance strains and human gastrointestinal floral changes

Intravenous Nutrition And Monitoring:

Reductions in surgical morbidity and mortality were brought about by advances in intravenous nutrition: In the early days, we had blood plasma, serum albumin, 0.9% sodium chloride along or with various concentrations of glucose, even high molecular weights dextran to improve patient circulating volumes in shock states. But, strides were made when companies developed protein solutions like animo acid-dextrose combinations and later a further advance by research ending in tolerable intravenous lipids that provided needed calories. A significant series of studies by Dudrick (x) whereby puppies were raised exclusively on transvenous nutrients, from birth to adult ages with no food by mouth, helped to establish this form of therapy. But the true value awaited new methods of delivery in people.

The problem was that critically ill patients soon ran out of peripheral veins to deliver fluids, and I really don't know who first used the subclavian approach to put a catheter in the axillary or the subclavian vein, but it was a turning point for nutrition therapy, all kinds of monitoring, and later even intense chemotherapy. So, in my mind, a simple little fixed anatomical technique whereby one waltzed a needle along the underside of the clavicle into the subclavian vein opened up millions of life saving procedures.

It also was the very foundation of innovative methods for evaluating central venous pressures and the popular Swan-Gans catheter that gave one fluid pressure values in the lung parenchyma – all vital for guiding fluid therapy in shock and toxic states. I can't tell you how many nights we sat up trying to decide about fluid therapy – to push or retract, under treat or overload, before these aids were introduced.

Heparin, Coumadin, And Anti Thrombosis:

A dramatic and frightening experience for a surgical resident was to have one of his patients die "before his eyes" with a massive pulmonary embolus.

This occurred on the female ward at Western Reserve during my training days. It was a long time 'til we figured out how femoral vein thrombosis, the seat of many pulmonary emboli, naturally formed during the stress and immobility of many operations.

And the discovery of a molecule, Heparin, developed by numerous individuals, and championed at the University of Toronto, counteracted blood clotting and thrombosis. Early in practice, we saw these blood clots as a relatively common complication, especially with hip and gastrointestinal surgery. We began using low dose Heparin with these operations and it reversed this trend. We also saw several examples where high dose intravenous Heparin immediately reduced the pain, improved breathing, and relieved distress of a dramatic lung blood clot. Utilizing the rat poison, Warfarin as Coumadin for long-term treatment to prevent clot extensions and enhance healing was also a positive step. And it took many years until we recognized the value of early ambulation.

Other Drugs And Modalities That Helped To Eliminate Surgery:

Toxic thyroid disease was a life and death problem during my training days but in early practice, there appeared a drug propylthiouracil (PTU) that slowed the pulse rate and allowed the only treatment then available thyroidectomy (operative removal of the near entire gland, leaving dime-sized nodules on each side). Not to be forgotten was "thyroid storm," a toxic state that required all sorts of tactics: surprise Avertin enemas, local ligations of thyroid arteries, finally ending in hazardous resections. We never had to do these maneuvers in practice because of PTU and drugs like propanolol, all beta-blockers.

The along came I-131, a radionuclide that selectively destroyed thyroid secreting cells and absolutely cured Grave's (hyperthyroid disease). It eliminated thyroidectomy as treatment for hyperthyroidism and also helped control certain metastatic thyroid cancers. Some initial enthusiasm was altered by the severe degree of hypothyroidism that resulted from theI-131, but soon was easily treated by thyroid extracts.

Basic Physics Improves Surgery And Eliminates Some:

The physics of transmitting light along glass fibers resulted in advances that enhanced some, but eliminated a lot of operative surgery. The first progress was with fiberoptic endoscopy that was a relief for many patients when a small fiberoptic, snake-like tube supplanted a rigid metal instrument. Dr. Orahood went to New York, and took a course from a famous Japanese endoscopist. Notably individuals from his nation were leading the world in this specialty at the time.

Complete exam of the colon and removal of multiple polyps by endoscopy surely prevented many cancers from developing and established the concept that polyps were often the forerunners of cancer. Upper, gastric, duodenal and even small bowel examination became possible. Dr. Orahood, with upper endoscopy, made a biopsy diagnosis of gallbladder cancer eroding into the duodenum, avoiding operation that we reported in the literature. Our endoscopy specialists began treating difficult stone impactions at the lower common bile ducts by sectioning the duct at the sphincter, opening the duct into the duodenum, with instruments through the endoscope, thus eliminating most indications for surgical operations on obstructive jaundice. They also would cauterize certain bleeding ulcers in stomach or duodenum and make diagnoses of cancer in the locations.

I hate to admit it, but the original operative intervention with fiberoptics was, in my memory, by gynecology surgeons. They did tubal ligations and removed ovarian cysts with intrapelvic endoscopy, and despite a few complications, they persisted and became the forerunners. The countless intraperitoneal even intrathoracic procedures, with helium gas, trocars, manipulating instruments, television screens, all beyond my expertise, followed.

Early Inroads On Cancer:

A development that changed the lives of nearly every female in our time was the Pap smear (by Dr. Papanicolaou, a Greek and American cytologist). Previous to this innovation, I had many disturbing findings in women with vaginal bleeding. Exam would disclose a fixed pelvis with cervical cancer necessitating only palliative procedures. After the Pap smear became advertised and popular, advanced disease became rare when replaced by early preliminary changes, easily treated with conizations and cauterizations.

Advertising and efforts by the state section of American Cancer Society led campaigns to get the idea of cancer out of the shadows into the open. There were many individuals in denial. For instance, several not wanting to recognize breast lumps until the problem was beyond therapy. Widespread information about self-examination, Pap smears, occult blood tests, not always perfect, but were steps in the right direction. Attempts at early diagnosis became a popular theme.

The same for the x-ray mammogram, which finally was shown to improve the overall survival of breast cancer patients by uncovering early, non-palpable lesions. The false positives were disturbing, but the concept proved to be reliable after decades of practice. We employed techniques with local excisions of calcified regions, then x-rayed the removed tissue to be sure we had included the particular calcified areas – a micro-stippled type of calcification was more often associated with malignancy.

A similar advance was when CAT (computer axial tomography) scans were introduced in the mid seventies by our x-ray department. This gave us tremendous vision over plain x-rays by adding a three dimensional picture, localizing abscesses, thoracic and abdominal masses, organ abnormalities down to the finest detail. It eliminated many observational operations and the rumor was about that it would reduce the need for autopsy.

A few mechanical devices that made surgery easier were:
1. The Kuntscher nail, an intra-medullary nail, for supporting long bone fractures. I went to several meetings on the use of this technique and we used them. They spared many patients months of overhead traction on bed rest. This method was the forerunner of all the intra-medullary pins and nails used in smaller bones as well.
2. A retractor that solidly fastened to the table and opened abdominal wounds for exposure better than any human assistant.
3. Mechanical staplers that we used to quickly close bowel ends when we did side-to-side or side-to-end anastomoses (hook ups).
4. Little things: small butterfly needles (with plastic wings) that gave us access to any small vein (very comforting and less pain for the patients in the middle of the night). Some of the needles came with thin plastic sheathes, an advantage over a rigid needle in a small vein.

The whole idea to dispose of used needles and drapes was born in this era – previously everything was sterilized and used over and over.

So, here we have presented some of the things introduced in our time, there being many more of importance in other fields with secondary benefits to surgery: anesthesia machines, polio vaccines eliminating whole hospitals, the same for tuberculosis institutions. Cardiac care and bypass surgery made possible by the heart-lung machine. Whole new specialties created by dialysis and kidney machines. It would be difficult to imagine an era more productive than ours, but there are endless journeys remaining.

The Scope Of Surgical Problems In Productive Years:

This chapter is replete with vocabulary pertinent to the practice of surgery, so I hope the reader will bear with me to understand many of the terms describing operations and diseases which they treated. These procedures are the excuses for the entire endeavor. Perhaps the complexities can be made more entertaining by my interjecting anecdotal incidents of human interest that stand out in my mind. These features were not prominent at the time of performance, but they stand out now, as I look back. Perhaps a glossary of terms or simple illustrations will help to portray the happenings?

Be advised that before the late nineteen forties and fifties, general surgery was a near-all inclusive practice. City hospitals had orthopedic, thoracic, genitourinary, nose-ear-throat and eye specialities, but county hospitals had few of these and no obstetricians or gynecologists. There was no oncology per se, cosmetic and bariatric surgery were unheard of, colorectal and hand specialties were yet to be recognized and curative cardiac procedures were awaiting by-pass technology. The chapter on training of the general surgeon further elucidates what we were expected to learn and practice. Basic skills were accented and we never heard of breast enhancement, fat removal or weight reduction operations.

County surgeons, for the most part, were concerned with life saving procedures, and there were so many that a try at categorizing them results in marked overlap, but a rough scheme follows:
1. Abdomen and perineum conditions
2. Cancer in breast and other regions
3. Trauma

4. Miscellaneous operations like thyroid, vascular, thoracic, skin and contents, plus extremities.

Appendicitis:

By far the most common abdominal operation we did was for appendicitis. It was a disease of the young, five to thirty years of age, but we saw a few people with the malady in their eighties, and some below the age of five. It presented with pain and tenderness in the right lower abdomen, often the organ was retrocecal (behind the cecum), but contrary to the norm we saw the disease confuse us by presenting in the upper abdomen, beneath the liver, in an inguinal hernia sac, or on the left side with situs inversus (reversal of position). Complications were frequent, like perforation with localized and generalized peritonitis, pelvic and abdominal abscesses that had to be drained with additional procedures weeks after the initial onset.

One case stands out in my mind, "was a real fooler", a patient of Dr. Stricker (he was always "bugging" me for something). He called and said, "Jim, this lady just delivered and she has more abdominal pain". Her white blood count was 18,000 and her abdomen was tender. This time he didn't have to talk me into operating. We removed a perforated appendix. The problem of right-sided abdominal pain at various stages of pregnancy was not uncommon, always added stress for all concerned, most we watched carefully and they got better. In some four or five with elevated white blood counts, we did appendectomies and fortunately we never lost a fetus, even when localized peritonitis was present.

I always had this "thing" about appendicitis that probably stuck in my mind, imprinted there when I was a high school boy, whereby our local hospital always had one or two young people on the wards, draining and dying from complications of this condition. And there's the young boy, early in my productive years, brought to our emergency room DOA (dead on arrival), sent home from another hospital for observation for abdominal pain. A lighter but personal story is that of my youngest son, crawled around the house with vague, on and off "belly pain" for weeks; we went to Children's Hospital in Columbus, tests galore, on to Cleveland Babies and Children's, more tests, psych evaluation of son and parents, no diagnosis. Several weeks later, more severe pain, vomited, high white blood count, gangrenous appendix removed, no more abdominal pain ever! Similar story with Dr. Kubiac's daughter: abdominal pain, GYN evaluation, observed at Indiana hospital, thinking it was ovarian problem, sent home, returned with perforation, multiple abscesses, three months later still draining, near death from repeated infection. The impressions of these cases and many more like them, made me eager about operating on young people with abdominal pain, even sometimes when all the salient signs were not present. In all the years, associated with this disease, we never had an in-hospital death save one and a tragic delayed complication, possibly not related to operation.

The first one was a 50-year-old obese man with peritonitis and septicemia, late in my career. He had all the modern technology, fluid monitoring with Swan-Ganz catheter, antibiotics, endotracheal airway management, acid-base control, and medical specialists, all to no avail. I remember vividly the many difficult days and hours of his ordeal.

The delayed complication was a young girl, the "pride and joy" daughter of a local doctor; her appendectomy went without incident and she was home, out of the hospital in three days. I remember her mom bringing her to the emergency room one morning, in a week or so after her discharge with vague symptoms and an attempt to get a urine exam with a catheter was negative. IV fluids were given and still no urine output. We took her to the kidney service at Children's Hospital, and despite weeks of intensive therapy, she died from renal failure. These were weeks of all-consuming ordeal for her family, mother, father and admiring grandfather. There was much speculation, but we never knew the exact reason for her kidney failure.

Tabulations of operations for appendicitis we did in my productive years showed some eighty to one hundred per year in the times from the nineteen sixties to the eighties; however, in the decades that followed, there was a gradual decline in incidence to about twenty per year when I retired. The reasons for this reduction in incidence were obscure, but we speculated that the increasing use of antibiotics by country doctors was a prominent factor. Colds and sore throats of viral and bacterial origin were often forerunners of appendicitis, and their treatment with antibiotics possibly averted obstructive lymphoid elements in the young person's appendix. Dietary habits, believe it or not, reduced hospital baby delivery rates, ten years previously were factor but never statistically proven. I garnered some data to show reduced monthly occurrences from the fiber, right after sweet corn season.

At a later time in the scheme of things, perhaps in the seventies and eighties, we began employing small bowel studies, barium enemas, ultrasound, and eventually CAT scans to help in acquiring diagnoses, but plain abdominal films were about as good as any, especially if one showed calcified fecalith (fecal stone). These tests were often disturbing to the sick patient. They helped sometimes in the individuals with a questionable story, giving patients and relatives the impression that everything was being done to avoid operation, especially in females; but the tests could never surpass history, abdominal tenderness and elevated white blood counts for diagnostic accuracy.

Conditions that mimicked appendicitis were frequently encountered: the list included ovarian problems like cysts with fluid or blood in the peritoneum, tubal inflammation or abscess, tubal pregnancies, endometriosis, urinary bladder cystitis and one strange perforated duodenal diverticulum that went retroperitoneal, making its way to the right lower abdomen. Twisted gangrenous omental tags were rare, but mesenteric adenitis with removable nodes for diagnosis was more common. We always tried to get tissue or culture fluids, some evidence to justify our operation, usually removing the appendix even if it looked normal. Mucinous tumors occurred, mostly benign, but a few spread about causing ascites, carcinoid tumors were not rare, sometimes uncovered only by microscopic examination of the organ, and causing concern for doctor and patient about advising, or not suggesting another more extensive procedure.

Last but not least to mention, there was a constant concern about our statistics showing the percent of appendices with no abnormalities that we removed. This number varied from year to year, but the patient with conditions that mimicked appendicitis was also included in this figure. We were always striving to conform to standards of the Hospital Accreditation Committee's examinations, balancing these with the patient's welfare. Even in the early years, there was a constant scrutiny of our practice, comparing our intended outcome with the final pathology and judging our results with those of other institutions.

Diverticulitis And Colon Cancer:

Diverticulitis and colon cancer were prominent diseases in our county. We saw an average of about ten cases of each per year for many decades. Every conceivable complication of these conditions, a blur in my memory, were obstruction, perforation, bleeding sometimes episodic, frequently presenting acutely, sometimes diagnosed by barium enema or rigid sigmoidoscopy.

A group of odd instances stand out from the many routine cases: I remember a town lawyer and his mother both came in with perforated diverticulitis on the same day. They both required temporary colostomies because of extensive peritonitis. We usually did temporary colostomies for any kind of colon perforation, with follow-up anastomoses (hook-up) in six weeks or so. Rarely then, but later on, with more efficient antibiotic use, we would risk a primary hook-up. I can't remember any primary connections breaking down or leaking. This problem was easily handled in the very rare perforations into the urinary bladder, this structure and the sigmoid flexure were often right next to each other.

My favorite general practitioner, Dr. Karrer, became the patient, and had an unusual perforation of a diverticulum on the right ascending colon that we were lucky to resect without colostomy. However, the sigmoid flexure was always the "hot spot" for complication, especially bleeding. Once, early in my career, I learned about seeking consultation from older surgeons. The patient was a ninety-year-old prominent local doctor called Daddy Longbrake with several episodes of massive rectal bleeding. The surgeon had done cases for Daddy in the past, and with the family's blessing, we let the patient die peacefully. But the consultant never looked at the record, never discussed the problem, and just talked to the family. I was hoping to get some bright insight about rectal bleeding, but got none. Deciding on the site and origin of rectal bleeding became an ever-present perplexity in practice, helped a lot by the introduction of an x-ray test with contrast injection, and we used a lot of tricks during operation to be sure of the site, not always successfully.

Cancer of the colon, often suspected because of test positive for occult bleeding, often followed by x-ray showing an apple-core lesion on barium enema, was often bizarre and complex. Contrast the case of my dentist, a former combat Marine who had been on Iwo Jima, came in with vague, minor abdominal pain, showed a small constricting area in the sigmoid by x-ray, and at operation we found inoperable tumor everywhere. On the opposite end of the spectrum, we had a one-centimeter diameter tumor in a woman resected after finding it by scope that we did because she had a previous breast cancer. At that time there was a current paper published showing an association of these two malignancies. Then, who could forget, another example of early detection, in a case of Dr. Karrer's, a farmer gored against a fence by his favorite ram, came with a ruptured spleen, had splenectomy, and after removing peritoneal blood, we palpated a small, solid, left colon cancer. It was resected a few months later, and he was thankful for his ram and the injury. Everyone agreed that early detection was one link in the chain for success against cancer but I know in my time most patients we saw had advanced disease (see chapter on surgical advances in my time). Advertising and changing the public image about the disease was a plus, but a vital positive link in the chain was deciding that polyps in the colon were forerunners of cancer.

We contributed to this notion when a patient wandered in to our hospital with familial polyposis, an inheritable condition characterized by a colon filled with polyps. We did a near total colectomy on this man, preserving the rectum, and a follow-up scope showed the rectal polyps disappeared after the low hook-up with the ileum. I thought this as some kind of miracle, and I called my friend, Jack Cole, (name dropping again), who was on the faculty at Western Reserve and later became the Professor of Surgery at Yale. He visited and we did many biopsies and numerous studies on this patient that led to cementing the concept that this condition led to ultimate cancer for these individuals. We postulated that something in the ileal contents led to the disappearance of the rectal polyps. However, the man lived in West Virginia, he came back for follow-up exam for awhile but eventually stopped coming, and I learned from relatives that he died of cancer. His son came for examination years later, but his scope showed no abnormality; he probably was only a carrier of an abnormal gene.

Another incident kept up our interest in inheritable cancer, when we resected a right-sided colon tumor from the father of our ward secretary. Right after his operation, the woman told me that her uncle, living somewhere in another state, had a similar operation a few months before, and that her uncle was an identical twin with her father. Wow, I got excited about this, and wrote to the other hospital, requesting records. They were very cooperative, sent path reports, charts and x-rays. The cancer in the uncle was a mirror image of her father's. I spent a lot of time writing about these cases, sent a letter to a local geneticist, but could never document the type of twinning. I got busy with other work and never published, but it was before the Lynch Syndrome of inherited cancer became well known.

As time went on in the late seventies and eighties, the number of colon cancer cases, in contrast to changes in incidence of appendicitis and diverticulitis, actually increased. One of the high points for me and our hospital was bringing a team from Ohio State University to Memorial; resect colon cancer after patients had injections of monoclonal antibody, cc49, labeled with 1251 to detect small deposits of cancer and lymph node involvement (see Research Chapter) with a Gamma probe. We did this several times and it gave our staff a feeling of being associated with a new and promising therapy.

James W. Sampsel

From the outset, my own operations for colon cancer copied those described by Dr. Turnbull of the Cleveland Clinic at the time: Always wide resection, removal of nodes to the aortic origin of the left colon blood supply, early ligation of the vein and artery in this location, and taking down the splenic flexure. We did this most of the time in viable patients, taking longer to accomplish but it had a better chance of cutting down on late recurrence. In the fifties, sixties, we did all combined abdominal-peritoneal resection for low lying lesions in the rectum, but later we did pull through operations, very low anastomoses from below, local excisions with supplementary radiation by Dr. GeBauer at OSU. We had a reasonably low incidence of post op leaking anastomoses with hand sutured methods, employed a lot of end-to-side hook-ups, giving a wide open lumen with a good blood supply to the margins. This technique was quickened when staplers came in and we used them to close the distal end of the proximal loop. We had the usual modest number of wound complications with abscesses and rare separations, despite our constant use of stay retention sutures, irrigations with Clorox solutions, antibiotics, and I was a constant advocate of inserting the intra-abdominal gastric tube for post operative suction on most abdominal surgery.

But one complication was completely unexpected: The patient was a nice sixty-eight-year-old lady, following a resection for colon cancer, was ready to go home, developed weakness in her legs and had difficulty walking. Things got worse. She progressed to complete paralysis of her extremities. We sought consultation with neurosurgery at OSU. Dr. Harry LeFever, the Chief, came and told us that she would progress to respiratory paralysis and the diagnosis was Guillain-Barré' Syndrome. We hardly believed him, but he was right on, and he mentioned she might recover, if we could get her by the respiratory paralysis. Of course, the only thing we had was the iron lung, the Drinker respirator, a barrel type enclosure, breathing maintained by a piston-like device, expanding the chest to inflate the lungs. Weeks of intensive nursing care and months of physical therapy followed. Eventually she fully recovered but rightfully complained of a sacral decubitus that was difficult to heal.

Some of the most difficult and trying wounds to heal were those from peri-anal and peri-rectal abscesses with their accompanying fistulae that required probes and setons to get repair while sphincter function was preserved. Several times I would send one of these patients to other surgeons at famous places, only to find the problems coming back to me unsolved. I did a lot of studying English texts by numerous physicians from St. Marks

Hospital on anal and rectal surgery. It's possible that their expertise was handed down, evolved, to them from the time of Henry VIII. St. Mark's hospital in London was the world seat of knowledge, no pun intended, for colo-rectal procedures. As a matter of interest, my friend, Jack Cole, who was previously mentioned, and later became professor at Jefferson and Yale, spent a year at St. Marks as an associate surgeon. I don't know where the common admonishing phase "you're a pain in the ass" came from, but in sessions with senior medical students, we always accented anal fissure as the number one cause of pain in this region. We always used conservative measures like dilatation, fiber diets, suppositories, but often ended up sectioning a portion of the internal sphincter transversely. Hemorrhoids were always a joy to take care of because the results were usually so good. I was always amazed how this one area would heal when you excised veins and lining mucosa in a longitudinal direction, leave a small section of mucosa intact, even with wide open raw areas lacking skin, in a region loaded with constant bacterial contamination, but it did. These patients were some of the most appreciative, including my own wife and our hospital administrator, Frances Helmick.

I'd like to, but cannot leave descriptions of conditions in this region without including rectal prolapse. Hemorrhoids pushing outward were simple, but I was startled when I saw the first rectal prolapse with six to eight inches of bowel protruding through the anal orifice. We did many different procedures for this malady, including excisions, hook-ups from below, plastic rings inserted behind the anus in old ladies, and several in young patients, from an intra-abdominal approach, pulling up and taking the prolapsed bowel somehow to the sacral periosteum that worked well.

Large bowel obstructions from cancer were fairly common, treated with a simple colostomy by a rod beneath the right transverse colon. The real toughies were old ladies with massive fecal impactions obstructing the colon, with the impossible task of removing from below and the morbid attempt of relieving from above. These and huge small bowel obstructions in old ladies, often with origin in minimal hard to find, inguinal hernias. Perhaps but I don't know for sure, that these horrendous cases were more prominent then, less so today, because of better social and nursing home facilities for the elderly.

I learned early on that small bowel obstructions, resulting from adhesive bands, were going to be a problem. Presenting with severe crampy pain, showing a distinct "ladder pattern" on abdominal x-rays, patients had standard treatment with nasogastric tube suction initially, sometimes resulting in improvement. However, often abdominal exploration was indicated to release the obstruction by severing adhesive bands. I learned some tricks of this maneuver, not from training, but from help of Dr. Maurice Zox, a surgeon from Columbus, mentioned in the chapter on physicians, with some early cases. He showed me how to move right in after large incisions, expose dilated loops, find distal collapsed loops and sever the bands, with hope that the bowel had not lost its blood supply. I was frequently an advocate of small enterostomy to decompress the distended loops with suction, and always a surprising amount of liquid here, necessary to be replaced by intravenous fluid. Crohn's disease with intermittent obstruction and resection was rare. I had several patients on steroids, one on methotrexate for Crohn's, intermittent with operations.

Hernia Repair:

I always thought it took me about five years in practice before I became familiar enough with inguinal anatomy to hopefully, properly, repair herniae. We did many hundreds, all kinds, big ones, small ones, incarcerated (stuck), strangulated (gangrenous with loss of blood supply) and I was enamoured with repairs utilizing Cooper's ligament (a firm fibrous band on a ledge of ileum, a pelvic bone), whenever possible. We did many with local anesthesia and later we used inserted mesh in one form or another. A lot of pediatric herniae were done by just careful dissection and ligating the sac, but my primary concern when doing babies was the difficulty with their anesthesia. Undescended testicle was frequently a problem with baby herniae that had to be dealt with. I got a call from some fellow, five years after I retired, complaining about a testicle that we salvaged when he was an infant.

Inguinal herniae in females were rare and frequently associated with some other anatomical entity, like a tube, ovary, or round ligament.

We reported a strange one in 1988 when we uncovered a hernia sac filled with thick mucous from a mucinous tumor, originating in the appendix. It took years of follow-up on this nice lady to be sure it was not recurrent. As mentioned, I learned early on to check the inguinal regions of any old lady coming from a nursing home with intestinal obstruction. The hernia repair was easy, but you had the problem resecting involved intestine without an additional large abdominal incision.

We struggled many a morning, well into the afternoon, with repairs of massive wound herniae, our own and other surgeon's. The fashioning of synthetic mesh into more of those repairs was a "God's send" for those patients.

Gallstones, Biliary Tract And Pancreas:

We had our share of patients with gallbladder disease, probably secondary only to appendectomy in the total number of operations, perhaps three or four per month, sometimes simple with pain and a few stones, often obstructed with acute and/or chronic inflammation, the latter making for difficult and trying procedures. The acute disease in high-risk patients was now and then treated with cholecystostomy, simple drainage of the infected and obstructed gallbladder employing local anesthesia. The real problem cases for deciding about operation were people with right upper quadrant pain and nominal or equivocal cholecystogram, our sentinel test, but diagnostic acumen improved when ultrasound appeared on the scene, identifying sludge and small stones. Our routine approach was: wide exposure, ligate the cystic artery, identify the cystic duct-common duct junction, ligate the cystic duct there, and remove the organ from below upward, rarely the whole procedure from above downward. I had challenging fun repairing several patients whose common ducts were ligated, once by an associate with open technique, and once by another surgeon employing fiberoptic cholecystectomy. They were both OK after repair. Fiberoptic cholecystectomy, whereby the cystic blood supply and duct are dissected out and ligated, employing a TV screen, is a routine procedure now, but one of the reasons I retired in 1996 was that I was too old to start training for this indirect type surgery.

The struggles we had with common bile duct stones were pretty much erased when invasive techniques of medical endoscopists became practical and they were able to enter the duodenum, section the Sphincter of Oddi and remove stones from below. However, in our day, we did cholangiograms, x-ray visualization of the bile ducts with nearly all operations for gallbladder removal. A small catheter was tied into the cystic duct before ligation, and radiopaque dye injected to visualize the biliary tree, showing stones or other defects within. If stones were detected, we would open the duct at a lower level, try to scoop them out with all sorts of fancy instruments, flush with saline under pressure, repair the duct around "T" rubber tube, and take another x-ray picture with dye, to be sure the duct was clear. Now and then, especially in a jaundiced patient, we need not have done all this, when after exposure, we could see the dilated ducts full of stone. This was the case of several outstanding instances: One was Reverend Hecker, a now deceased minister of St. Johns Lutheran Church, a lovely structure sitting at a cross-road in the country. One of his sons became General Hecker, the commanding officer of the Ohio 37th Division in WW-II. The same situation, the common bile duct full of stones, occurred in Dr. Callaway's wife Ethel. She came in after Fred was treating her with medicine. He was afraid of having her operated on because several patients of his died after gallbladder operations in Columbus hospitals. When we did Mrs. Callaway, removing her common duct stones, she "never turned a hair" meaning she did OK. Stones were not always removed as easily as they were in Ethel, especially when they were impacted at the lower portion of the duct and the sphincter. This required opening the duodenum, something we did not like to do in the high-risk patient, severing the Sphincter of Oddi, and removing stones from below, just like the endoscopists did routinely years later.

A final word has to be mentioned about a few impossible problems we saw involving the bile ducts: Fibrotic stenosis of the entire ductal system, where the structures were thin, contracted, obstructed, and we're still confused about the etiology here, probably an auto-immune phenomenon. Then there are also carcinomas arising in the ducts or the gallbladder. In the former, we palliated with bypasses one way or another, but in the latter there were several surprise cures when only microscopic pathology revealed the diagnosis, after routine removal of, what we thought, was inflammation. Most prevalent was gallbladder cancer beyond the operative stage, and we had a case report published in Surgical Rounds, with Dr. Richard Orahood, showing a chance biopsy of a patient with one of these advanced neoplasms by fiberoptic endoscopy. It was not a world-shaking discovery, but it was a plus for Memorial Hospital.

All the known maladies of the pancreas were seen during my tenure at Memorial. We had lots of acute pancreatitis, some chronic disease, cysts, endocrine tumors, and frank cancer. The latter was frequently treated by a simple exploration and biopsy; because the disease was usually spread beyond the limits for operability. I remember one in the father of my automobile dealer and another in Ethel Callaway, Fred's wife, whom we did common duct stone extractions some twenty years before her cancer developed. She had symptoms, we explored, biopsies, decided it was inoperable, far off relatives came, took her to OSU, saw Dr. John Peter Minton, re-explorations, same opinion, no further therapy. But there was another lady that had breast cancer and I will include her full story later, but she developed abdominal symptoms years later, we explored, biopsied, got a diagnosis of adenocarcinoma from a mass about the pancreas, thought there was nothing more to do. They went to OSU to Dr.Minton, re-operation, new diagnosis was breast cancer with involvement of nodes about the pancreas, improved on anti-estrogen therapy and she was angry with me, rightfully so, but pathology also could not tell the original biopsy was breast cancer. So here, I was only batting 500. Yes, we did about three Whipple operations for early pancreatic cancer, two of them in conjunction with Dr. Orahood. They all did fairly well post op, but all died within a year with metastatic disease. I had better luck with a benign pancreatic cyst resection from the pancreatic body and tail.

Acute pancreatitis was a medical problem when simple, and only required nasogastric suction with support. But when it presented as advanced and progressive, the fullest surgical armamentarium was necessary not only to combat shock and toxicity acutely, but also to deal with drainage of cysts, with tubes, fistulae and often small bowel anastomoses, accompanied by the maximum in long-term intravenous nutritional support. We had several of these that we were almost ready to give up on, but they persisted and survived. One was the mother of our public relations officer. Chronic pancreatitis was a different ball game, patients with severe back pain we usually sent to OSU, after getting some new operations they would often return with pain, candidates for psychotherapy, addiction, too bad there were no pain specialists then!

Gastric And Duodenal Ulcer Disease:

Of all the conditions that contributed to hospital occupancy, duodenal and gastric ulcer disease were high on the list in the first few decades of our institution. This made so, in part, by our initial treatment for acute symptoms, hospitalization to remove patient from stress situations, diet and antacid therapy around the clock, sometimes constant drips with gastric rubes and tranquilizers, all for a week or so, before considering operation. Pain obstruction, bleeding, perforation were the main complications that dictated operative intervention. Early on, all our operations for ulcer disease were gastric resections. Our so-called understanding of ulcer etiology was that of increased acid production by cells in stomach glands, and removing a large portion of them was the correct therapy. This principal was strongly prompted by one Bill Abbott, an associate professor at Western Reserve, sanctioned by us in training, publicized in national journals, emphasizing that some 90% of the stomach mucosa had to be removed. He had such a fixation on this concept that he had us measure areas of resected stomach, make a map on paper and compare amounts removed with results. Restoring the continuity of the GI tract was established by about four different methods, most using the jejunal portion of small bowel, sometimes duodenum, but the latter being difficult to fashion without tension.

We did all of these procedures, most turned out well, some not so good. Lots of folks had had ulcer disease in those days, one of our bank presidents had one of these resections for obstruction and he was ever grateful. Maxine, the wife of Dr. Stricker, one of our general practice doctors, had a gastric ulcer that required resection. We thought the etiology of the ulcer was because she drank twenty cups of coffee every day. My accountant had a resection with fabulous result for ten years but required re-operation. The recurrence rates were minimal but metabolic problems with nutrition deficits, weight loss, were sometimes a complaint.

One case, etched in my memory, that turned out "not so good" was that of Virginia Smith, a young woman with ulcer disease, had resection, recurrence and secondary operations, ended up with no stomach, massive adhesions, and we constructed a pouch of jejunum connected to her esophagus but she still had obstruction. She didn't want to go, but I sent her to Dr. Jeff Gordon? at OSU, and she improved after his procedure. I remember his words when I called and apologized for sending him this difficult problem: They were:" Don't worry, I'm a big boy and I can handle it". I have used this phrase several times since then, in tight situations. Virginia has a lot of stress as a teenager when alledgedly, her mother subjected her to men, for hire. Stress was accented again as a raiser of gastric acid by Dr. Hans Seyle in a tome on the subject, many years later work on physiology by Dr. Lester Dragstedt and others, at the University of Chicago, became practical in the form of vagotomy and pyloroplasty for duodenal ulcer.

We began using this procedure sometime in the late sixties, removing vagal fibers from around the esophagus and enhancing stomach emptying with pyloroplasty, severing the pyloric sphincter. These innovations gave remarkable ease to our operations for ulcer, reducing time and manipulation, giving less complication, reduced recurrence and practically no nutritional difficulty. Furthermore, it was possible to utilize vagotomy even in the presence of certain perforations, to help in reducing recurrence. We did this in one famous case of Tom Hurd, our chief x-ray technician, who had a horrendous perforation, survived, gave me and his medical consultant the ultimate praise: "If I get sick again, and you are no longer here, I will just let nature take its course". And this, no doubt is just having faith in the doctors you know.

The number of operations we did for ulcer disease dropped suddenly from the average of 10-15 per year, until about 1980 and beyond, falling to one or two. The last I did was a Japanese fellow that had rapid bleeding after a fiberoptic biopsy, a dedicated worker at Honda, did not want to take days off from work for an operation. We had to call his mother in Japan, using an interpreter, get her to urge him to accept our recommendation. He finally consented to a life saving procedure. He was one of two that year, the marked reduction in ulcer operations therein resulting from the introduction of acid reducing drugs, H_2 blockers and Proton Pump Inhibitors. The slower notoriety of ulcer treatment with antibiotics came along with causative Helicobacter Pylori was described early in the next decade.

Gastric cancer was rare in our county, two cases in some forty plus years, one inoperable in a middle aged woman, another in an old man that was curable. The idea of the time was that the incidence of this tumor was decreasing worldwide. No one knows why? A far out thought would be that the same organism causing ulcer, Helicobacter Pylori was shown to be present in most gastric cancers, and was being treated inadvertently by wide spread use of antibiotics? We had one big carcinoid tumor of the stomach that had bleeding and bone formation within the mass, a patient of Fred Callaway. We reviewed the literature and reported it in the American Journal of Surgery in about 1972.

Breast Cancer And Others:

If there was one operation I hated to do, even worse than leg amputation, was radical mastectomy for breast cancer. Throughout many decades, we followed the dogmatic principle of William Halstead, the father of American surgery from John's Hopkins, remove breast with wide skin incision, take off muscles over the rib cage, pectoralis major and minor, dissect lymphatics and fat tissue off the subclavian vein, artery and brachial plexus, close the wound, apply suction tubes under the flaps, and hope for the best.

Of course you had to remember that in Halstead's day, and also in our early years, we saw mostly patients with advanced disease, frequently ulcerated big masses, axillary tumor, requiring careful dissection, often followed by advising radiation to the area. But we were also confused and saddened by the not too rare case of a young woman; small-localized tumor, no axillary spread, and dead in 6 months or so, despite radical operation.

Sometime in the seventies, we were introduced to needle biopsy of breast masses that gave us an advanced impression as to whether the lesion was cancer or perhaps a benign cyst. With the help of the pathologist, we would insert a needle into the mass, apply suction and get enough tissue for a diagnosis. Of course we would have an opinion from examination, but the needle biopsy often confirmed our opinion and gave us information to discuss with the patient and her family.

Sometime in the seventies or early eighties, also a momentous event occurred at one Saturday Morning Grand Rounds; it was Dr. Zollinger, (then present editor of the American Journal of Surgery), wanted an opinion from the group if he should publish a study submitted by a North Dakota country surgeon. The article showed, in a small series of women with breast cancer having only localized excision of tumors, a similar or better five years survival than those of a comparable group done with radical operations. The comparable group was a historical study, done in the past, and was a "no-no" for statistical comparison, but around that time came many similar studies that firmed up the data. Thank the Lord, or someone; I began early on to do localized excisions of many breast cancers. Very soon it was shown that the recurrence rate was reduced by combining localized excision with post operative radiation, and that margins free of tumor in the excised specimen was also a key to a low recurrence rate. It has to be mentioned that at conferences and rounds many chief oncology surgeons denounced local excisions, but later on, when the concept was well established, no one admitted being wrong, of course!

About then, along came the mammogram, a specific x-ray study that took years to establish as a factor in reducing the mortality from breast cancer. We all learned to read them, and along with x-ray folks, we did innumerable local excisions of early cancers, along with many thought to be cancers that turned out to be benign. We did a lot of these excisions with local anesthesia; something I never liked to do for fear of spreading tumor cells about with injections. Breast abnormalities demonstrated by mammography were frequently marked by fine wire, dye injections or often we just excised a quadrant containing the defects, the latter was my favorite, especially if the defects were in the outer quadrants, then taking the quadrant specimen to x-ray for a picture to be sure the abnormality was excised. No matter what was the substance of adverse criticism of early mammograms, like too many benign lesions excised, x-rays causing cancer, cost, or pain of the procedure, eventually they proved their value, not only for enhancing survival, but contributing to the biological knowledge surrounding breast cancer. It gave us the idea that some tumors were slow growing, could sit for years with "carcinoma in situ", many pre-cancerous lesions identified, cysts defined, benign adenofibromas outlined, and who's to know how many excised benign lesions would have turned out to be bad?

We never needed x-ray help to diagnose inflammatory breast cancer; a specific entity with a very bad prognosis, characterized by an entire breast involved in a red, solid, tender mass. Two of these we saw early, did mastectomy and they did not survive long. The third came along later and there was evidence to treat these pre-op with chemotherapy and anti-estrogen therapy, which we did, successfully. However, this was the lady that was angry with me; because some years after her breast incident she developed a pancreatic mass that we thought was pancreatic cancer, on further surgery by Dr. Minton, turned out to be treatable metastatic breast cancer. It was just after the work of Dr. Huggins at the University of Chicago suggested that tumors were influenced by hormonal elements like testosterone and estrogen. Tamoxifen, an estrogen blocker, came on the scene along with chemotherapy, and we gave both for many years until oncology clinics were established at Memorial. Many patients that we sent to the oncologist came back to us and complained about their scientific discussions being too realistic concerning patient survival, but they had to discuss the good and the bad.

One final note is worth mentioning about breast cancer: In the twenty or thirty years Dr. Karrer and Dr. Ingmire treated women from the Amish community, we never had one with breast cancer, nor did they have cysts, pain or mastitis, that was frequent in other women. We never knew for sure why this was, but they all had multiple pregnancies, all nursed their babies for years and I guess they fit into the popular epidemiologic studies then showing these features were somehow associated with low incidence of cancer.

We saw an abundant number of other cancers, Hodgkin's disease in young people, retroperitoneal sarcoma in one of our valued practical nurses, a reportable spreading, basal cell carcinoma in an old man, many muscle sarcomas and an outstanding case of bone sarcoma that we did a hind quarter amputation with the help of Dr. Art James, the founder of the James Cancer Hospital. Art James was a great friend, and I called him many times early on to get advice about patients with various cancers. He was instrumental in the treatment of a famous case of melanoma survival in a young woman with metastatic disease that we gave continuous intra-arterial methotrexate. I called him and he said: "Jim, we have this new drug called methotrexate and you might as well try it". We had a new technical advance, a chemofusor pump that would deliver a given dose of medicine intra-arterially that we had used at Reserve to treat head and neck cancers with temporary success.

Squamous cell tumors on lips of farmers were pretty common, most were big time smokers, and in the sun all day. I got pretty good at excisions, many times rotating flaps hanging on circumferential arteries. Nose and face lesions were excised with skin lines being used to advantage in scars, often using split or full thickness grafts from behind the ear to match face skin. Many of these plastic procedures were ably taught by one Daryl Shaw, my favorite Cleveland plastic surgeon, who was always in trouble with nursing and the professor at Reserve, discussed in the chapter on training. Dr. Shaw gave me a small plastic needle holder as a gift for being his resident that I treasured for years. There was none like it on the market.

One other episode involving tumors was that of a three-year-old boy of Dr. Ingmire's that had a bump on the left rib cage. We removed it to find one of the bizarre childhood lesions, very aggressive, a myosarcoma, or a non-differentiated sarcoma that showed local spread in a month or so. We discussed the case with Dr. James and our x-ray physician Dr. Riebel. There was a fellow at University, recently trained at Memorial in New York, whose expertise was implanting of radon seeds within plastic ribbons, into spreading cancers. He thought this would be a good case to apply this technique after repeat resection. We brought the child back, resected involved rib cage on the left, and he applied the ribbons about the entire left chest. The boy did OK, and the ribbons were removed at the proper time. I can't remember how many days? Twenty years later this patient showed up at Memorial to show me how ribs were absent on his left side, and I had trouble remembering the details, but he was thankful for remembering the trouble he went through. It illustrated for me, once again, how we were lucky to have the technology of the University and outside world at Memorial.

I really enjoyed the dissection necessary to remove mixed tumors of the parotid gland. There was the initial concern with the wide exposure necessary and the fear of injury to the main trunk of the 7th facial nerve with the initial uncovering, followed by handling the small peripheral branches surrounding the tumor. We saw several invasive cancers of the parotid gland that destroyed the nerve even before our operation. The results were pretty horrible and they still haunt my memory. Nerve grafting was then in its infancy.

Sections, Ob Complications, Gyn And Others:

General practice physicians did all the obstetrics at Memorial in the first three decades; they delivered all babies. Dr. Stricker probably the most, Dr. Butler delivered my youngest son, Dr. Karrer delivered many women from the Amish community at their home, and lots at the hospital. The overall number delivered was one a day, about 365 per year, accompanied by a low complication rate and an acceptable section rate. I can't remember ever losing a mother during these years. We, like many other institutions at the time, were constantly balancing the health of mother and child with the ever-present accreditation surveys. I should mention that we never lost a mother after section surgery and the only baby we ever lost was with one instance of acutely ruptured uterus from a longitudinal section scar, done elsewhere. The patient was brought to our hospital in labor, and the uterus ruptured as she was wheeled into the operating room. We opened the abdomen with local anesthesia, but the baby was dead. We had one other close call after section when a mother developed "red shock", we stayed up all night with her, me and Dr. MacIvor, controlled pressure and respirations, and we were lucky she survived.

Anesthesia was always a tricky problem with sections, we did not want to put the baby to sleep, so we had to move along, perhaps five minutes or so from initial incision, to extracting the baby. Longitudinal uterine incisions became a "no-no" early on, and the operation was "speeded up" by low transverse entry after elevating the bladder flap, the latter also gave easier wound closure and less chance for complication with subsequent pregnancies. One problem we had extracting the baby was in one of our OB nurses, of all people, a tight squeeze resulted in a fractured arm for her baby – fortunately, it healed promptly, but I never heard the end of this one!

A consultation that created some wonderment on my part, early in my career concerned a labor patient of old Dr. Marsh. She had good x-ray measurements that suggested normal delivery, but progress was slow and getting critical. I was puzzled so we asked a Columbus obstetrician to come and give an opinion. He had delivered thousands of babies, many by section. He entered the hospital in a flurry, never looked at the patient, the chart or the x-ray, just "Bring her in for a section". I helped him; the whole thing went with local anesthesia, done nicely. Never worried about our section rate, and I was impressed. As my own career went on and on for twenty years plus, and I was privileged to do about two sections on women I had delivered by section, many of my actions became somewhat similar to his.

The practitioners recognized and called frequently for opinion on pre-delivery bleeding from placenta previa that we handled in various ways, the most severe requiring section. One time at delivery, we had a uterine prolapse with massive bleeding that we replaced from below and did an immediate hysterectomy from above. There were all sorts of problems with dead intrauterine babies that I prefer not to remember. How did we handle them and deal with anxious families, I'll never know? A few aborted somehow but rarely we did hysterotomies or extractions from below. I always wondered how these were handled in the days before frequent hospitalization? Not so good I'll bet!

Most of my experience with gynecological procedures came from my time in the military when the hospital at Ramey Air Force Base was my assignment in surgery. We had a fellow captain, Don O'Connor, M.D., married to Lolita, a Puerto Rican girl; he was way ahead of his time with sections and hysterectomies, as we handled these problems and surgery for a good part of the dependents from the Caribbean Command and often the natives. Don was eager to have me help him with his surgery and he needed lots of assistance with fluid, blood and infection difficulties. But, as it turned out, the confidence and the operative moves I learned from him became valuable at Memorial; because, at Western Reserve, in my training, general surgery and McDonald House, the OB and GYN facility, had a unwritten pact that said: No taking each others patients, and they were completely divorced. I often wondered about that.

So, at Memorial, for two or three decades, I did all the tubal ligations, tubal pregnancies, endometriosis problems, pelvic repairs, hysterectomies, D&C's, cervical biopsies and conizations, a few radium insertions for cervical cancers, assisting Dr. Riebel, our radiologist and radical operations for same. Life was made more exacting for me by some of the rules we abided by at memorial, for instance, before we did a tubal ligation, we had to have three signatures on the chart of the patient that the operation was necessary. The same for hysterectomy. This was a "hold over" from a rumor previously held that our hospital sponsored the idea of "uterless Union

County". As you will see in other chapters, this rumor made it difficult for me with the American College for good or bad.

Uterine bleeding was a constant dilemma for us, and I was amazed how the D&C would make a diagnosis and often cure it at the same time. Dr. Lloyd Barnes, a Columbus Gynecologist came and operated on my wife Dolly for this, and we called him for a few confounding situations after that, getting him to like our work place, for more frequent consultations. He taught me how to do vaginal hysterectomies, but I was never comfortable with this procedure, preferring wide exposure offered by the abdominal approach, often visualizing the ureters in extensive resections, and there were many, with football sized fibroids.

One complication, that still haunts my dreams, was postoperative vaginal cuff bleeding. One or two required re-operative ligation of the hypo gastric artery in the pelvis.

Ovarian cancer was then and still is now, a "sneaky disease", difficult to make a diagnosis until it's out in the peritoneum. We were lucky to find the rare case of ovarian cancer with a localized mass that could be resected for cure. More often it presented as abdominal enlargement, and I remember improving a few of these patients with our first chemotherapy, nitrogen mustard in 1954.

There were so many other accounts of our delving into female maladies, I have lost many details, but one stands out so that I cannot exclude it: There was a stately, middle-aged lady, called Hazel, in town that did abortions for hire by inserting elm sticks into cervices; we finished a few of them after bleeding and infection supervened. She was ahead of her time, having a product in beginning demand even then. She was always well dressed, proud, went to church, and was rumored to be a girlfriend of a local dentist, lived in a modest, neat house. All the doctor's wives shunned her – but she was nice to my youngest son and he liked her, almost everyone knew about her, but somehow she was never prosecuted. She faded away in the late sixties and early seventies, never having had the benefits of Roe vs. Wade decision decreed by the Supreme Court in 1973. I remember completing uterine clean out of a few patients with her attempted abortions or others with spontaneous incidents having massive bleeding. Small fetal parts coming out intact, a few still moving was always a surprise. We had no thoughts about doing abortions on demand; we were always tied up saving lives.

It was in the next decade or so that a crisis was arising within our hospital administration, doctors, and all of us over the status of our obstetrics department. General practice doctors were getting older, many were giving up their enthusiasm for delivering babies; several other county hospitals had closed their obstetrical units. We thought it would be a mistake to close ours, so Dr. MacIvor and I made valiant efforts to acquire specialists to take over these endeavors. We thought it would be natural for the University to assist us with this specialty, perhaps send a fellow or resident or provide us with physicians finishing their training; because we had a considerable volume of patients, and it would also be a financial benefit to the University. However, we got the "run-around" from the department head there, Dr. Fred Zuspan, a Union County native, and I'll never know why. We'll discuss it at length in another chapter but meanwhile we obtained Dr. Roger Parenteau and later Dr. Larry Gould to lead our obstetrics and gynecology practices, relieving me of a great burden that for years was an intricate part of this country surgeon's life.

As a counter-measure to bringing in babies, and as a means of helping to reduce the world's population, we did vas ligations. The vas deferens can be easily picked up, isolated on the side of the scrotum's loose skin, fixed with towel hooks, severed, and the ends carefully ligated. The vas is rock hard to palpation, compared to the testicular artery and vein, which you do not want to ligate. There were few complications, but we always pointed them out to the patient. One was the fact that he was not sperm free for perhaps six weeks after the procedure. We quit doing these procedures after a while, because I never really liked to do them, too many times they were associated with marital infidelity. It was interesting to note, no outside doctor permission was necessary for vas ligation but we needed three doctors to sign for tubal legations.

My training on the genitourinary service came in handy for problems like testicular injury, testicular torsion, and diagnosing testicular cancers. We had our share of these, one in a local physician. The ultrasound test came in and really helped make diagnoses and reduce the rate of exploration. There was special concern of young people and their parents over these lesions.

I became an expert in inserting a Foley catheter and many times used filiforms and followers for prostatic obstructions. We did several suprapubic prostatic resections for obstructions before the days of GU consultations, and it was amazing for me how the prostatic bed healed around a Foley catheter.

Other Procedures:

The second operation on the list that I hated the most to do was leg amputation. I had a good start with handling this disliked procedure: because, our chief and professor at Western Reserve had a classic paper in the American College Journal describing a simple and quick method for above the knee amputation that received international notoriety; big skin flap anteriorly, sever tendons, dissect and isolate the major vessels behind the knee, insert a Gigli saw to sever the bone just above the joint, rotate the lower leg and you're looking at the major vessels and nerve for easy ligation, sever the posterior muscles to be fashioned over the bone, remove the leg while leaving a big posterior skin flap, ligate a few small bleeders, close everything up, and that's it. The tough part was the back and forth movement with pressure and counter pressure necessary to cutting bone with the Gigli saw, one of man's greatest inventions of a stout, rough wire, with two handles, that would cut through anything if used properly. I learned from one of our nurses that if I hummed or sang a song while doing this, it relieved some of the anxiety always present for me in this phase of the operation. We did many above knee amputations in older folks with diabetes and vascular occlusive disease, below the knee in younger people for trauma or rarely infection. We always used amputation as a last resort, and usually with physiotherapy helping in the post-op care, with an eye toward prostheses whenever possible. Would you believe, we did a few cross leg flaps for big lower leg or foot defects in young people, requiring cross leg casts for weeks in the hospital. How they tolerated these, I'll never know!

Before we acquired the superior vascular surgery services of Dr. Bill Smead and Dr. Pat Vaccaro, both from the University, we managed to do a few peripheral and aortic bifurcation endarterectomies. It was a time when peripheral vascular disease was very common, and we were fortunate to have a fellow from radiology, brought by Dr. Frank Riebel, Dr. Bill Molnar, who migrated from Europe, working at the University. He was one of the pioneers in devising methods to visualize coronary arteries, but for us, he would inject dye into the femoral system and visualize the extremity vasculature, showing areas of obstruction. We had some success opening arteries and stripping lining atheromata. We also used the Fogarty catheter for opening acutely thrombosed vessels. This catheter was a great invention; you inserted the thin catheter beyond the obstruction, blew up an attached balloon, then pulled out the catheter, dilating the vessel and extracting the blocking thrombus. And whoever heard of a procedure that we did once in a while for cold extremities from ischemia called lumbar sympathectomy. This was a general surgeon's dream; because he was delving into the neuro and vascular field, patient placed on side, flank incision, reflect the peritoneum and abdominal organs, isolate the sympathetic chain beside the vertebrae, resect a small portion of the chain, close the wound, and hope for a warmer extremity. We usually did a local anesthetic block of the area to show some benefit before advising the operations. We also did stellate ganglion blocks in the neck for arm dystrophies; these blocks also sometimes helped ischemia in the fingers, and they were relatively simple to do by inserting the injecting needle against the transverse process of the 7th cervical vertebra.

An extreme unusual vascular case came in early in my career, George Jelen, a man with a sub hepatic mass that at exploration turned out to be a false aneurysm of the hepatic artery. Now, who ever heard of that? Well, we reported on one six years earlier when I was a resident. For George, we occluded the artery, excised the aneurysm, and repaired the vessel. But it recurred in a few weeks, we went back in, tried to repair the vessel with cellophane covering, and it recurred again. I lost a lot of sleep over this case; we were afraid of ligating the artery, fearing hepatic necrosis, we finally had to ligate the hepatic artery, and instead of the hepatic necrosis we got duodenal necrosis and George died. He was a courageous fellow, and you can't believe how brave he was through all of this. I thought about sending this man to the University, but my opinion was that he would do all right with us, especially since the last one I saw at the University was diagnosed at autopsy.

We did another false aneurysm, this one of the aorta that was man made. I placed a small catheter in the side of the aorta as part of a procedure for metastatic melanoma, whereby we gave continuous Methotrexate, and six months later a mass developed that was a false aneurysm. Dr. Dick Orahood and I repaired it with a vein graft support. It remained intact for the life of this nice lady.

The most frequent vascular procedure that we did in our time was for varicose veins. An initial problem with this malady was deciding for patients for sure whether those distended leg veins were the cause for symptoms like fatigue, swelling, pain, leg weakness and ruling out other conditions was paramount. But seeing folks with non-healing leg ulcers, marked pigmented and edematous skin improve after operations was worth the effort and time they suffered with surgery. We had a set of tests and tricks to evaluate the competence of the deep leg veins and perforating branches, it included dye injections for visualizing the system, and knowing of these branches and ligating their connections was a feature that helped prevent recurrences. The sites of these connections were marked with pencil or scratches beforehand.

The operation started in the groin with careful dissection to identify the saphenous-deep vein connection, ligation of all the small branches off the area and most importantly, double ligature on the saphenous vein just where it joined the femoral. If there was one salient feature of the procedure, it was this, visualize this junction for sure, and ligate the saphenous vein without interfering with the femoral vein lumen. Next, we went to the medial, inside of the ankle and inserted the vein-stripping instrument as far as it would go, rarely right up to the ligated saphenous vein in the groin. There is a wide attachment to the insertable blunt end that allows the wire to be pulled out from below, pulling the entire external superficial system, and its branches with the device, of course, including the varicosities. Most times, the instrument had to be inserted segmentally, removing portions of vein at a time, the curvatures and even a few remaining valves would interfere with the instruments' complete passage. Pulling out the wire with the veins was the hard part; sort of like using the Gigli saw to go across bones. Multiple thuds as the branches were pulled loose were disturbing, and it helped to hum a tune during this phase.

We always worried about the bleeding that would occur into the tissues when the veins were pulled out, but it was never a problem when we applied local pressure. Sew up the wounds, apply extensive dressings, apply Ace bandages, and have patients return in about two weeks. Most of the time, they would be happy with the results, rarely a single varicosity would remain for injecting sclerosing solution, but I was not happy with these injections, especially when done just for cosmetic indications. Also, rarely there would be some numbness along the inside of the leg from peripheral nerve injury that would clear up or become less noticeable in the ensuing months.

Acute and chronic deep vein, femoral vein, thrombosis was an ever present dilemma for us, with patient edema, sometimes non-healing leg ulcers. The best therapy was long-term conservative measures with anticoagulant drug, compression bandages, and elevating legs. I do remember ligating a few vena cava's for recurrent pulmonary emboli before the days of the insertable vena cava filters.

James W. Sampsel

Thyroid Surgery:

Our county being in the goiter belt, we had a variety of thyroid disease all the time. The gamut ran like this: Massive benign goiters, small thyroid nodules, toxic hyperthyroidism, tumors like papillary or follicular cancers, even a few fatal undifferentiated cancers. We did thyroidectomies frequently for Grave's Disease, toxic hyperthyroidism, before I-131 became popular as medical therapy. I had an advantage with thyroid surgery given to me from a fellow, Dr. Brown Dobbins from City Hospital in Cleveland, came to University, was dedicated to teaching thyroid surgery. He passed on his principles to all the surgical residents, and I'm sure they go on and on. For me they were: careful dissection of the whole gland, leave a thumbnail portion on the trachea, identify and preserve the recurrent laryngeal nerves, see it enter the larynx, identify and preserve the parathyroid glands. But like in ski or tennis lessons, when you teach ideal moves, one also has to deal with non-ideal conditions, and they frequently occur during operations. Sometimes you had to pray and think that, even though you didn't see parathyroids, some were left behind. Or ligating that last bleeder close to the trachea, you didn't really catch the laryngeal nerve. For the last quandary, it really made one relieved if all the vocal cords were proper when they were viewed by final laryngoscopic exam.

The number of our operations for hyperthyroidism decreased rapidly when I-131 became the primary medical treatment for toxic thyroid conditions. The beta-blockers like Propylthyiouracil and later Metoprolol Succinate, were highly essential for reducing the hazard of "Thyroid Storm", and later were used as long term medical therapy, but I-131, one of the only radioisotopes to enjoy widespread clinical application, proved to be the first choice of most patients for cure. Nevertheless, the principles of thyroid surgery applied, especially with removing large goiters, and especially when treating cancers.

The so-called papillary cancers were prominent in young people, usually confined to one lobe, but sometimes extending into the mediastinum. I couldn't believe when one of these patients with such very advanced disease would survive and be O.K. for years. Follicular tumors, frequently confined to a lobe would usually require total thyroidectomy, metastatic spread was unusual. But the undifferentiated cancers were all fatal, one in a woman from the Reformatory, another in an older man that lived locally; no surgery or chemotherapy was of value. A significant advance came about when we introduced needle biopsy to thyroid nodules. With the help of the pathologist we could place a fine needle into the nodule, aspirate tissue, and many times decided in advance, cyst, benign or malignant diagnosis. The number of thyroid operations we did continued, and I helped the new surgeons, Dr. Pelfrey especially, with cases right up 'til my retirement.

Trauma:

When I review the times we had with the squad bringing people to our emergency room, never turning anyone away, rarely sending patients to other institution, I wonder how we achieved the status of first, second and third levels of trauma care. There was no such thing as these levels of care then, so I guess we had little or no alternative, but remember, as part of my training with Claude Beck, we would incise the chest and massage the heart directly to enhance circulation, so we did a lot less dramatic resuscitory measures like external cardiac pressure, airway clearance, central lines for fluid transmission, stopping bleeding and so on. We took a lot of people directly to the operating room for intra-abdominal and chest emergencies. Some of these stand out: One quiet Sunday afternoon a Jewish family from New York was driving by route 42 and 33 intersection, a location about five miles from us, and from where we got numerous patients from a steady stream of accidents. This family was hit by another car, all were injured, husband, wife and two children. We admitted them all to the hospital; the husband was the only one seriously injured with an intra-abdominal emergency. When I told them that an emergency operation was critical, they were skeptical because of my youth and we were not a big city hospital. Dr. Maurice Zox, a Jewish doctor from Columbus, who I describe in another chapter, saved the day, when he came and told them that I was qualified and he would help. We operated to advantage, fixing a torn liver and other bleeding. The patient survived, stayed for a few weeks and went back to New York to rehabilitate.

A young man from the adjacent state of Michigan was in an auto accident and was brought to our emergency room in shock. Blood loss was the cause and we explored the abdomen right away. Spleen, liver, mesenteric vessels were all intact, after removing blood and clots, we found the source in a small artery still spurting, beneath the liver, and we ligated two free ends. When things were cleaned up, we were able to examine the area closely, isolating the hepatic artery and the offending vessel, torn in two, with free ends ligated, was a branch of the hepatic. We looked up the anatomy, and decided it was the gastro duodenal artery. The surgical literature had several other publications describing this injury, but they were extremely rare, and we reported this one in the Archives of Surgery. It seems that this structure, in its course from its branching to its ending was positioned over a vertebral body, and a shearing force disrupted the vessel.

Another bizarre happening in a 6-year-old boy with a swelling and redness over his left cheek, thought to be an abscess by his physician, was opened in his office and blood spurted across the room. He applied pressure and brought the child to the emergency room where we ligated the facial artery at the angle of the jaw. All the wounds eventually healed. It was a spurious aneurysm of the facial artery, described many years ago in sword playing athletes, where a small lateral cut in the facial artery results in a hematoma, which eventually turns into an aneurysm. The six-year-old boy had blunt trauma two weeks previously when a tooth lacerated his cheek, with a through-and-through injury that was closed with a few sutures by his physician. Was this a chance happening or what? Here was a boy from little old Richwood with the same type of wound common to ancient swashbuckling, French swordsmen.

Trauma to the spleen, with or without fracture of the tenth left rib, left shoulder pain, peritoneal signs from extravasated blood, falling hemoglobin, shock, all indicators of splenic injury, the most common major abdominal catastrophe. We saw all the described: damages, fractures, tears, complete fragmentations, all with massive blood loss, and early on these emergencies were trying for me. However, each one was a separate case and the general principles were the same: Replace the blood loss, and in a few we filtered blood sucked out of the peritoneum, reinserted it via peripheral veins along with transfusions, wide exposure, clean out clots and blood, grab the spleen and curtail the bleeding. Things got a lot better when I learned to isolate the splenic artery and vein just above the body and tail of the pancreas - thus stopping all the bleeding. This maneuver also helped when we had other splenic pathology like Felty's Syndrome, and Idiopathic Thrombocytopenic Purpura cases that we did later on in conjunctions with the medical oncologists. It was in one of these patients that we first gave pneumococcal vaccines, when the idea became popular that patients with removed spleens were susceptible to pulmonary infections by certain pneumococcal organisms. The concept was advanced that patients, especially young people, should be observed rather than operated upon right away for splenic injury. Fortunately, I never had to deal with this dilemma, because we never had a case of splenic injury that we could observe with confidence, and later on, many of the serious injuries were sent to Columbus by helicopter.

All the instances recorded in this book have random components, but some more than others. One of these involving splenic fracture deserves telling: It was Saturday morning, clear and crisp, on my way to the hospital for rounds, at the corner of 8th street and Grand Avenue, our hospital administrator, Frances Helmick, was driving in the opposite direction. We stopped and chatted. Her son, Bill had been injured in the football game the night before, taken out of the game, went home to bed, and I asked her how he was doing? She said: "He's OK, but he doesn't feel well and he's having a lot of pain in his left shoulder." A light went on in my brain, and I said: "Take him to the Emergency Room, I'll be right there". Sure enough, he had all the signs, abdominal tenderness, falling hemoglobin, and his abdominal x-ray actually showed a fractured spleen. The organ has a huge central tear, bleeding profusely before removal. We reviewed the game films, identified the very play where he caught a knee in his left upper abdomen and lower chest. Now, who's to say he would have survived another night at home with increasing blood loss? We'll never know, but we were all happy the way it turned out!

An intra-operative problem, not related to the spleen, that I had not seen before, as a result of bizarre pressure effects within the abdomen, during automobile crashes, occurred in the number two Methodist bishop. At our emergency abdominal exploration, we found a perforation at the cecum, but the entire right colon, even part of the transverse had the outer muscle layer near completely separated from the inner circular muscle, leaving a thin mucosa exposed in other regions. We thought about resecting the entire involved colon, but decided to repair the defect by attaching the outer muscle layer back into its original position. We repaired the big cecal perforation by bringing out a cecostomy. He had a stormy postoperative course and after a few days, he was transferred to Riverside. Probably, we should have resected the involved colon and done an ileostomy instead? But, we'll never know, and I never saw or heard of this problem again but in retrospect, I doubt if this damaged bowel would ever function properly.

The urinary bladder was the object of blunt trauma when a tree fell on a nice lady. She and her husband were out in a new property they had acquired. He cut down a tree and it fell on his wife, knocked her down, and she came in with abdominal pain. The intra-peritoneal portion of the ladder had a four-centimeter tear that we repaired in layers and inserted a Foley catheter in the urethra to protect the suture lines. Another small puncture wound of the bladder was repaired after a young woman had a tubal ligation at another institution. The early abdominal surgery done with fiberoptics, nitrogen expansion to the peritoneum, the Gynecology physicians started one of two small portholes for instrument entry. They were the first ones to insert scopes into the pelvis to make observations on ovarian pathology, and early on they did tubal ligations in this manner. In this unusual case, the woman returned home from one of the procedures, but had increasing abdominal pain, and we thought it was from bleeding, but it turned out to be a small puncture in the urinary bladder leading urine into the peritoneal cavity, easily repaired.

Union County had primarily farming communities and the hospital collected numerous patients from farm accidents, by far the most common was associated with corn picking. For many years in corn harvesting season, we treated arm and hand injuries that you can't believe! Men would get corn stalks stuck in the mechanism, it would stall the machine, they would reach in to free the block, and get their hands or whole arms stuck in the inlet when it suddenly started up. There were several instances where they would be stuck this way, out in the field, for hours until someone rescued them and somehow freed their extremity. Typically, we saw degloving type injuries where skin and subcutaneous tissue pulled off hands, arms, tendons exposed and damaged, fingers partially amputated, whatever. We did a variety of maneuvers to treat these injuries: Complete amputations, grafts, abdominal full thickness flaps were the natural covering for many. All the training I had with Daryl Shaw's plastic surgery came in handy. To illustrate again how chance events can influence behavior, all these corn picker accidents stopped when someone invented a device to shut off the motor when the operator left his seat on the picker. With the mechanism shut down, no more accidents, stalks released, motor starts again when the operator gets into the seat. We saw a lot of bizarre accidents associated with mowers, riding and push mowers. Once a piece of metal flew out from beneath a mower to get stuck in the thigh of a near-by patient.

Several foot injuries that got caught in a push mower came in. Someone was always running a tractor on the side of a hill or a steep grade and having it turn over on him or her. One such accident was fatal for a young woman brought in with irreversible shock, blood loss from a major wound in her back and buttocks. Somehow the tractor ran over her, deeply detaching back muscles along with skin and subcutaneum. We took her to the operating room, the bleeding had stopped, her blood pressure was zero and it stayed there despite fluid and blood administration. She was a patient of Dr. Ingmire's from Plain city and one of the only patients to die in the operating room; perhaps she had some other hidden injury that was never uncovered?

Dr. Kubiac, our orthopedic consultant arrived just in time to fix an injury in my oldest son, Jim. He and his brothers were fooling around with snowballs and he stuck his hand through a glass door, sustaining a deep wound of the wrist that severed multiple tendons and the ulnar nerve. This was a devastating injury for his being involved deeply in high school basketball and football. At the time of the injury, I was operating on some other case, and they came to the door and said" "You son is in the emergency room with a deep laceration of he wrist." I said, "Call Dr. Kubiac", and he took hours to repair it.

In the decades before we had orthopedic services, I did all the fractures, arm bones in kids, femurs with overhead traction in special beds, open repairs of tibia fractures with plates and screws, but I was really happy to attend meetings about and use intra-medullary nails and rods when hey came in about that time. I was pretty good with plaster cast technique, but the master of this was Dr. Willis Kubiac who will be described in another chapter.

My favorite fracture to fix was the prevalent hip injury in old folks. We used the Smith-Peterson nail for breaks at the femoral neck and added plates with screws for inter-trochanteric variety. Our technique was fairly simple, anesthesia, fracture table, maneuver the hip to fix the alignment, incision, insert a stout wire into the femoral head, x-ray picture to be sure wire is properly placed, then drive the flanged nail with central hole, over the wire into the femoral head, not too deep, just solidly into the head. This is all we did for neck type fractures, but for inter-trochanteric types, we added a plate attached to the nail and fashioned it onto the outside of the bone with screws. The latter type fracture usually healed well, but in time we learned that the neck injuries, despite perfect pinning, ended up with necrosis of the head, because the blood supply to the head was altered and disrupted by the initial displacement. Neck fractures were soon treated by orthopedic specialists, inserting titanium head and neck implants, eventually complete hip replacements. Willis Kubiac could pin a hip in about thirty minutes, but it always took me several hours. I was happy when he took over the entire fracture business but I continued to handle some of the less dramatic surgery like tendon repairs, occasional tendon grafts, excisions of massive rheumatoid nodules about joints, and joint infections of various types. Twice we saw massive joint infections where x-ray revealed a small, thin sewing needle within the knee joint cavity, and the patient had no idea when or how the needle got in there.

A most dramatic and anxiety filled prospect for a patient is when there is an airway obstruction that restricts breathing. In my training days, we saw this as a frequent problem on the NET service with croup type laryngitis in children. The general rule, as passed on from Val Jordan, the department head, just returned from four years in the south Pacific, was: If they had skin retraction above the sternum with respiratory effort, and if you were in doubt, do the tracheostomy, for if they had continued struggle, fatigue would take over, they would become lethargic, and tend to stop breathing entirely. Inserting a tracheostomy tube to give someone access to breathing is a relatively simple procedure. Perhaps the most difficult part is holding down the anxious and struggling patient while you block the skin and tissue over the trachea, make a longitudinal incision over the trachea, below the thyroid cartilage and above the sternum, enter the trachea with an up and down incision, cutting across tracheal rings, spread the wound and insert the curved tube. There is usually tremendous relief from the patient as soon as the trachea is opened. Minor bleeding will occur, but in the exact midline, it will be minimal, sometimes small vessels need to be ligated. The metal or plastic tube for insertion at the tracheostomy was a great invention, curved so that the open end slips right into the opened trachea, with a proximal flange so that it rests on the skin around the neck wound. The tube has an inner compartment for periodic removal and cleaning, should be examined and handled by everyone who may have the opportunity to use it. It was a primary operation for all senior students to learn in the dog lab at OSU in past years.

At Memorial we had occasion to do tracheostomy multiple times, two or three in an emergency, and others for long term problems of comatose patients in the ICU that required respiratory assistance with pressure machines and endotracheal tubes. The latter, placed through the vocal cords and larynx has an irritative effect when used for long term, and the tracheostomy device with removal inner component, is much more efficient for cleaning and maintaining an infection free airway after even a few days or a week.

The first emergency was a fellow that fell forward on his wheelbarrow; his neck hit the sharp backside and fractured his larynx. He came in with great respiratory effort, controlled but getting worse, no chance here for an endotracheal tube, and he was immediately helped by a tracheostomy tube insertion, done carefully and slowly. Another was a middle-aged lady, known to have multiple allergies, suddenly had breathing difficulty, brought to the ICU, had medical therapy with steroids, insertion of endotracheal tube attempted, had edematous larynx, not improving, anxious, struggling, retraction with efforts, tracheostomy with tube, immediately relaxed and breathing normally.

All of these patients can have the tube partially obstructed and eventually removed if and when their primary problem is resolved. Removal restored their ability to talk; the wounds usually heal completely, when covered by a simple dressing.

A third example was a real emergency: Patient was in the O.R. for an abdominal operation, anesthesia, in the form of Ben jie Hoagland, had administered initial pentothal and curare, the paralyzing drug, usually no problem with inserting the endotracheal tube for pressure ventilation; it didn't go, I tried with no luck, Carolyn Ziegler came in and tried, no luck, we did immediate tracheostomy in a hurry, anesthesia proceeded, and operation followed. Some fun! The patient woke up after surgery, not being able to talk, but accepted the explanation about the emergency with no thought of legal action against us.

Another breathing problem common and usually dramatic, with pain and anxiety was a pneumothorax, (collapsed lung) spontaneous or from depressed rib fractures. Treated by inserting a needle followed by a catheter on high suction to the pleural space. The lung collapsed and the mediastinum can shift to interfere with blood return to the heart. Heavy suction in the pleural space usually allows the lung to come out and stick to the parietal pleura. Sometimes it took days and rarely we had to send patients to University for thoracic exploration and resection even, especially if there were multiple blebs on the visceral pleural surface in smokers.

Burns:

This is one form of trauma that hardly ever has a perfect ending. Fractures heal, ruptured spleens are resected, lungs re-expand, but sometimes death is the best answer to severe burns. The scars are forever present, not to mention the psychological scars present surrounding the initial injury and repair. Yet many people that we saw, depending on the severity, after months of operations and healing, got back to a relatively normal status. I learned early on to use the Paget Dermatome, another fabulous invention, to cut skin at various thicknesses, and also to use another great device, the skin spreader to enlarge the original graft so that it covered more area. We adhered to the old concept of letting third degree burn damage mature, late debridement under general anesthesia, then graft skin onto healthy granulation tissue. We had a special bed for burn patients that was a great innovation, frames and support front and back, able to rotate the body back and forth, no need transfer to the operating table, anesthesia, and débride on one side, turn the patient over when necessary to get grafting skin, turn back to apply it. Of course, the loss of fluid and electrolytes, frequently underestimated in severe burns, had to be replaced, and there were formulae that were based on the percent of body involved plus the extent of burn depth. Keeping up urine flow, kidney function, combating infection and shock required constant expert nursing care initially, before operations could even start. Many of these girls that were involved in this care are described in the chapter on Nurses.

One fellow we got back to a fairly normal life after months of pain and stress was a school teacher from Milford Center, had a high percent of body burns, all third degree, maybe four or five operations for debridement and grafting, depression overcome, finally walked out of the hospital. Another was a lady of Dr. Calloway's, smoking in bed, fell asleep, third depress about 20% body surface, same scenario, depression, wanted to die, multiple procedures, was finally discharged to a still troubled life. Numerous other extremity, low percent, second and third degree damage, some even débrided and grafted, initially in the hospital, later treated as out patients.

A few more are etched in my memory as bad: One was a young man overturned a motorcycle, gasoline escaped, ignited, came in comatose, work up, third and fourth degree charred all over, died in four or five hours, asked for a cigarette in his last hour and he smoked it. We could not find a place to insert an intravenous line. We injected morphine through charred skin and made him comfortable. Another tragic case was a middle-aged colored lady, auto accident, car caught on fire, she was rescued but had extremity burns, and one leg was third degree. We treated in our usual way, planning on a late debridement. She was from the Chicago area and wanted to be transferred; we were happy to send her to another hospital by ambulance. A few weeks late, someone from the Chicago hospital called me and said they had to amputate her leg. This hit me like a "bolt from the blue", but I did remember that she had an inordinate amount of pain in that burned leg. Probably the superficial charred and extensively burned skin interfered with the blood supply. Possibly, extensive longitudinal incisions in the charred skin would have prevented the leg from ischemia, but who is to know for sure! Several papers appeared in the literature, about that time, discussing this problem of vascular compression by tight, charred, burned skin, and the therapy was immediate, bold, extensive incisions in this offending surface covering. I was always looking to do this and never had another opportunity. One reason was that burn centers became popular in the sixties and seventies, one opened at Ohio State University and we were more than happy to send all the severely burned patients there for the specialized care they needed.

Here we are at the end of describing the procedures that occupied one country surgeon for some forty-five years, and I guess you could say: The random events that led to his productive state of life were mostly in my favor and gave excuse for writing this book. No way could I include all the intriguing incidents related to the surgery, and many will appear in other chapters. As mentioned, they were all happenings at a given time and place, probably duplicated frequently by other surgeons in the same time period, but not likely before or after these decades. I have tried not to fall into the old, frequently described psychological trap, of remembering the good and suppressing the bad and some of the bad has been described in the human interest chapter, all headaches and heartaches.

Also, I hope the regulatory agencies like The American College of Surgeons or The Ohio State Medical Board will not be adversely critical of me for trying to express personal ideas, utilizing multiple plights of my patients, who came to me for operations in good faith, thinking that their maladies would not be advertised. In most instances, names were not mentioned. Where necessary names were changed, and the few left in, I know would be happy to be included.

Research, Surgical And Other:

There is exciting wonder in the human mind for pioneers that seek the unknown, be it with the limitless concepts of outer space, the universe, or the less dramatic microscopic and sub-microscopic world of biology. In a sense, with regard to surgery, each basic discovery, like in chemistry, physics, biology of the immune system, even the genome project, all may improve the specialty, but many modify the field with intent to rightfully eliminate it. For the individual researcher, the journey into the scientific project is all encompassing, carrying out the plan, testing the hypothesis, gathering in the data, all are paramount. Strangely, arriving at a conclusion can be anti-climactic, and usually only suggests another endeavor.

For me, research being supplementary to the main task of country surgery, I look back, and there are numerous thoughts that come to mind: first, is the emotional high, emerging from the simple idea that each days work in research often revealed something that no one in the whole world had ever seen before. It sounds naïve, but for me this was true of every project, in every laboratory, alone or in conjunction with compatriots. There was always the eagerness to examine today's slides, or seeing the results of today's reactions, record these advances, for tomorrow we try a different tack, a different concentration, vary the operation, be sure to examine the control carefully, and how does today's discovery fit in the overall scheme? It can be likened to a lottery, whereby one has the idea that today's small discovery could "hit the jackpot" with world-shaking possibilities, another spoke in the wheel to understand or benefit some destructive human malady.

A more practical second aspect of research lies in its ability to enhance understanding of many entities related to surgery: shock syndromes, massive infections, wound healing, respiratory and metabolic problems, to name a few. The very act of doing library, now computer, searches of the literature on a given subject, delving into the basics, often leads one to acquire confidence for a given clinical path.

Research During Training Years:

Research paths tend to move from one accented modality to another, through decades of time. This fits into my own involvement in the discipline, whereby early on during training and early practice times, with the basic sciences, chemistry, biology, physics and advanced instrumentation developing, case reports and collections of surgical problems were popular. We reported rare spurious aneurysms of the hepatic artery, made several unsuccessful attempts at repair, before learning about simple ligation, which was made possible by advanced methods of displaying positive collateral circulation to the liver, and/or the use of new antibiotics, both acting to prevent liver necrosis.

Frank Barry and I encountered a rare jejunal ulcer in a patient with very high gastric acid values recurrent after gastric resection. This was before Zollinger and Ellison described their syndrome caused by a pancreatic tumor producing gastrin. (The ZE Syndrome was a landmark discovery, showing how a tumor could produce a substance with untoward secondary effects). I traveled to Elyria, a Cleveland suburb, to investigate our patient's autopsy after she died there with ulcer perforation. We photographed and studied the findings, probably completely overlooked the causative pancreatic or duodenal tumor later described by these physicians. We also reported on a very small kidney tumor, from the G.U. service with Dr. John Williams, when early discovery of cancer in the individual patient became an essential goal.

Dr. Bill Holden, the then Chief of Surgery at Reserve, wanting to help stay abreast of the new trend in basic type research, assigned residents to basic science projects and I got paper chromatography, a new means of separating serum proteins, as my appointed deliberation, but I was then tinkering with a method to do a rapid serum amylase test for pancreatitis, so little thought was given to the former. I had this crazy idea that one might quickly evaluate serum amylase from a patient, exposing it to a starch solution, running the mixture, timed, through a capillary, fine glass, tube system. It was a great quick test, very sensitive, but after months of work, with the chemistry and dynamics of starch solutions, I abandoned it for a chance to work with DNA in a real laboratory.

James W. Sampsel

What Was This Dna, Deoxyribonucleic Acid?

About then, there was a surge of activity and interest in DNA, deoxyribonucleic acid, as being the universal substance in all living things, a concept now and then contested, but being pretty well established. There was a rumor about some lady in Pathology working with methods to estimate DNA in cells and we had to submit a plan for our six months research project, which needed approval first by the Chief of Surgery. I had this "far away" idea that the rejection phenomenon of homografted skin had some sort of causation in the DNA and DNA would react differently in auto-grafted vs. homografted skin. (The term homograft in those days applied to a graft from one individual to another. For some unknown reason, this term homograft has been supplanted by the term allograft, which is now in use for transfer of tissue or organs from one individual to another within the species. Grafting from one species to another is designated as xenograft.) Another reason for my choosing this project was the anticipated advantage for use of the Padgett-Hood Dermatome, required to make all the skin transfers. I also had this far out, "naïve idea" in the back of mind, concerning a remote possibility, working with the rejection phenomenon and DNA, might lead to some connection for cancer therapy.

The most prominent research person engaged with DNA activity at that time in our institution was Dr. Cecille Leutchenburger. I got an appointment to see her with the request that my project from surgery would be carried out in her laboratory. She was a German-Jewish lady, about five foot six, glasses, with a bun of dark hair streaked with gray. She pursed her lips frequently, always questioning, confident, sometimes smiling, not accepting my request at first presentation, but on a second appointment she approved with admonitions: that I would adhere to the rules of the laboratory, not consider the project a minor endeavor and not abandon research, but continue it in some form after leaving there. I agreed to all these principles, while thinking she must have this idea about surgeons being wild and egocentric, not to be trusted in the confines of a research laboratory.

Her first suggestion, which in retrospect I should have heeded, was for me to do the project using mice instead of dogs. However, I already had the animals lined up in the surgical dog lab, anesthesia alerted,

Padgett dermatome ready to do the grafting, so we started with two dogs transferring autografts and homografts (allografts) on each.

The basic work and the main thrust of activity in her lab at the time was measuring the relative quantity of DNA in the nuclei of cells, stained by the Feulgen reaction, (the Feulgen reaction was a chemical method with a dye, to stain DNA exclusively in cell nuclei) then recording light absorption, through a cylinder of an isolated nucleus at 1,000x magnification. This was all done in a dark room with a sensitive photometer and the light source was of an optimal wavelength, 554 mμm (millimicron) using a Wratten filter. Sounds complicated doesn't it? Well, it was, but we showed results from our measurements correlated with a biochemical estimate of DNA in liver cells, done on similar tissue in a joint project with other laboratories. They were measuring amounts of DNA in millions of cells, but we were recording values in individual nuclei.

The activity was exciting everyday for a novice fellow like me, collecting data, producing histograms of haploid, diploid, aneuploid nuclei, beautiful green visuals through the microscope, correlating amounts of DNA with the constantly dynamic cell activity in the grafted skin. Our work helped establish the concept of DNA build up in the diploid nucleus for mitotic division and later work describing the polyploid abnormal nuclei of cancer. Of course, this notion was suggested by untold numbers of pathologists for years, with routine methods of staining but our lab established a quantitative aspect to DNA in the nucleus, enhancing the thought of DNA measured increases leading to mitoses, the production of two cells from one.

Associated with work on my main project in the lab, we engaged in numerous side efforts: for one, we applied our method of measuring DNA in nuclei of dog skin as it deteriorated, incubated in saline, within a Petri dish, on the lab windowsill. We were surprised to find little change in values for weeks, indicating that DNA maintained integrity, at least to our reactions and measurements, longer then we anticipated.

More significant was a simple small study on wound healing in mouse skin, employing a new stain of Dr. Roy Korson, a cytochemist friend of Cecille's. The stain combined Orange G, Methyl Green and Toluidine Blue in a reaction that showed dynamic changes over time in protein, DNA and RNA in the wounds. And on serial sections, glycogen was demonstrated, by the PAS reaction, to be in high concentration, a new and important finding. This series of experiments turned out to be most significant, at least it got us a presentation at the Cytochemical meeting in New York, where we all went, and where I learned to like Chinese food, at the urging of Dr. Leutchenburger.

There were other projects going on in the lab. I helped with a few, closely observed and thought about others like the study of lung changes in rats exposed to cigarette smoke, a classic of its day, showing progression from inflammation to cancer in bronchial epithelium. Another study in progress showed the formation of multiple nuclei in giant cells were macrophage in origin. This process, the formation of giant cells with multiple nuclei that occurred in tuberculosis and other diseases was made clearer with this information.

We were also intrigued by a phenomenon that occurred after we conducted partial liver resections in mice to obtain cells for our studies of DNA measurements. Weeks later, in mice that survived, repeat examination showed liver size had returned to normal. This was regeneration secondary to function that we only wondered about but it helped to foster studies of a phenomenon repair after destruction by diseases in that organ.

All part of the picture were associations with the overall workings of a tidy and efficient research lab, with a confident, stern but understanding director, weekly lunch meetings to discuss findings, and monthly conferences reviewing the literature, individual assignments, often presented at the director's home.

Not to forget the personalities of other folks in the lab, the Chief Technical lady, Ethel, a middle aged, hard of hearing lady, taught me everything about mouse anesthesia with small ether cones, tissue fixation and preparation for cutting sections, complex math calculations, and insisted I pronounce the word data, with a hard accented "a". She thought anyone that pronounced it with a flat, dat-ah, was a "dumb-head". She also hardly mentioned it when I almost blew a hole in the high ceiling of the lab by throwing a just extinguished match into a big waste basket, which contained ether soaked cotton balls from the morning's operations. I really hated to leave the daily routine of the research lab after six months there, but it merged into the pathology service, and for a few weeks back and forth was easy; because both activities were in the same building.

I leave my epoch in this lab with a few more connected thoughts in my mind, after these many years: one good one is that several surgeons from our University service went to Cecille's lab for research after I left; mostly they concentrated on DNA in cancer and their work was significant. Another set of innovations, not in our lab, but right around the time we were struggling with estimating DNA in grafts, two British scientists

Medawar and Billingham, in 1951, had discoveries showing graft rejection to be part of a new concept called the immune reaction. The other exciting, world-shaking feature of these years was the chemical and crystallography exploitations by James Watson and Francis Crick to uncover the double helix conformation of the DNA molecule. This led, through the next few decades, while we were operating on people everyday, to untold numbers of scientists uncovering details of the four DNA nucleotides, labeled T,A,G and C. There followed the isolation of the very gene coding for the MHC, the major histocompatibility complex, some fancy term, eh? But this was a distinct marker of early individual's cells, and this knowledge was essential to the ultimate success of transplantation through matching donors and suppressing immune reactions with drugs.

So, with regard to our own research efforts with DNA in grafted skin cells, data collecting, paper writing, never accepted, its effect on the practical aspect of transplantation, none! As a primary exertion, you might say, all bad, but secondary associated activities, and a pleasant journey, all good.

Reseach Mixed With Practice Activities:

The next adventures in our research effort starts with a tale of my dear wife carrying in the back of our station wagon, a cage full of white rats, which she picked up for me, at a railroad station, in some back alley, a tough neighborhood in Columbus. Now this is hard to believe, but there were times that I could not leave Memorial, even for a few hours, and we got the word about the rats being delivered and they had to be picked up - today! This was an especially scary venture for my wife, Dolly; because we then had temporary quarters in a country farmhouse where "beedy-eyed" brown rats stared at her from wall pipes, as she added coal or removed ashes from a basement furnace. However, she got the rats home, fed and watered, ready for the project. Unlike their relatives in the basement the inbred white rats were placid and well-mannered animals.

The plan with these creatures was to evaluate changes in small bowel cells (mucosa) after massive resections. About then, the mysteries of regeneration in liver, kidneys, and small bowel were being thought about, and I had this burning desire to study this process because of a recent case we had, showing survival after extensive small bowel resection, and there was a quandary about the possible changes in remaining loops of bowel accounting for continued absorption of nutrients. I could only study the gross and microscopic morphology of these changes in rats, and eventually

Guinea Pigs. The latter all began screeching whenever you entered the lab with a head of lettuce. I learned to know all the animals, rats and Guinea Pigs alike, hating to harm them, but there was no other way. With ether anesthesia, resect 50% to 80% of the small bowel quickly, fashion the hook-up by telescoping one loop into another with a few tacking sutures, return the animals to cages, observe for two weeks or longer, reoperate and study the remaining loops. They were always enlarged to gross observations. An interesting observation was also made when a major portion of small bowel was by-passed and not removed. The functional loops enlarged, but the by-passed loops remained small and developed packed luminal debris from continued shedding of their lining epithelium. The landmark series of experiments reported about that time, concerning intestinal lining cells, was by a fellow named Charles LeBlonde at McGill University in Canada. He showed by injecting tritiated Thymidine, and utilizing autoradiography on tissue sections, that there was a constant dynamic movement of cells from base to apex of the intestinal lining. I remember attending a surgical meeting in Montreal and going to McGill to see LeBlonde's lab. It provided necessary enthusiasm for continued work on my project.

And it required lots of enthusiasm for removing enlarged loops, fixing, clearing, embedding in paraffin, cutting my own sections, staining, measuring cell numbers and sizes. All this was done in the upstairs rented portion of an old house; the downstairs being my practice office at the time. One of the biggest problems I had was getting alcohol for preparing tissue sections. The ATF department agents visited me several times to be sure I was not selling the stuff or creating a bomb. I ended up using Methyl instead of Ethel alcohol. Finally, sections were produced for microscopic observations from the enlarged loops for measurements. The conclusions were that the remaining loops had increased function through both hyperplasia and hypertrophy of individual cells.

But, you guessed it! We never had anything published about our work on small bowel regeneration despite the fact that we showed the morphological basis for increase in function. Submitted papers were rejected several times with interesting comments from reviewers like "This is an interesting work but requires more statistical treatment", and so on. Once again the journey was fun, and we never really arrived.

Another series of practice related enterprises that often raised the ire of nurses from the OR, especially Mrs. Bowman, when I set up an apparatus in the clean-up room to inject India ink into appendices and/or the arteries of resected colon tumors. Many removed normal appendices were going to waste in Pathology, so I decided to inject lumina with India ink via a pressure canula. The ink appeared in the serosal lymphatics with low pressures, and this gave evidence to our concerns for leaking of toxins or bacteria to the peritoneum in the right lower quadrant as early and frequently occurring in appendicitis. Further, when the slides were returned from Pathology, we were able to show the path of bacteria and the inflammatory reaction through the wall of the organ

With colon tumors, we did arterial injections of India ink into the cancer and the surrounding normal colon, confused the Pathologist, but it displayed many interesting features of tumor and normal colon blood supply at a time before Dr. Judah Folkman put forth his concepts of angiogenesis. We all had these far out ideas about the blood supply of cancers being important items for study and therapy. It was our pleasure many times after that to see and meet Dr. Folkman at OSU conferences, being his family lived in Columbus. His life and work were role models for everyone at the University.

Surgical Applications For The "Magic Bullet", Research At Osu With Monoclonal Antibodies (Mab's):

How the numerous random events insinuated me into this research group at OSU is complex, but it began somewhere around the sixties and seventies, with Dr. Orahood, a friend and a practice colleague, having connections with Dr. Ted Martin and a private research company known as Neoprobe. Dr. Martin was an associate on the faculty in oncology surgery at OSU and was working with the new concept of injecting monoclonal antibody, labeled with a radionuclide, 125 I, to mark small and large cancer deposits for removal during open operation on patients with colon involvement. The cancer deposits were being detected by a sensitive Gamma Probe, which was invented and developed by Dr. Marlin Thurston, a retired Professor from the Engineering Department at OSU. Dr. Martin encouraged my input and I became enamored with the whole exciting possibility, delving into the complex pathology of cancer, working with patients, associated with untold numbers of learned individuals. This was a world-class group with multiple disciplines, basic research aimed at practical clinical achievements, essentially financed partly by the University and partly by private capitol from the Neoprobe Company. Encouraging academic and private industry cooperation was just then coming on strong.

We were part of specialization necessary for the ever-expanding state of knowledge, made so by multiple individuals with multiple disciplines necessary for each step forward. Of course, in country surgery you had the instruments, anesthesia, nurses, surgeon and assistants, but it was a relatively simple life saving endeavor. But here, for the research path, you had surgery, plus expertise of engineering for the Probe, immunology necessary for the antibody, chemistry for attaching the radionuclide, obtaining permissions from committees and patients, tolerating Pathology input, statisticians, medical writers – how Dr. Martin corroborated all this, I'll never know! In a world where everyone's ego is on display he never received enough credit! I distinctly remember one conference we had, where the then Chief, Dr. Olga Jonasson, expressed the idea that our effort merely established a new way to stage colon cancer; while our thoughts, entirely different, involved a complete new approach to understanding the disease, ultimately leading to therapy.

As I look back on all these differing opinions, the anticipated importance of all the activity, the advantage I had was similar to that of my strictly clinical faculty advantage. I was an outsider, looking in, making some contribution that allowed attendance at meetings, discussions, presentations, but having no financial or other responsibility, or rewards.

One of the distinct pleasures of being remotely part of this effort was the association engendered with great people: Dr. Ted Martin directed the project, and I guess you could say my whole involvement was due to his tolerating my input. We traveled to meetings at Princeton, Johns Hopkins, Los Angeles, Washington, and NIH, always of the same mindset, rarely disagreeing. Ted was an enviable expert at Tennis, played varsity in college, had a court in his home grounds, always played at your level until it got close, then he'd turn it on! Frequently, we were the only two surgeons in meetings with other science people, and it is where I learned from him to begin any comment with "I'm just a simple surgeon, but"-.

Then there was Dr. Thurston, about my age, but I always thought of him as an elderly gentleman, brilliant, versed in quantum physics, inventor of the sensitive Gamma Probe, involved in the basics of developing fluorescent nano particles, emeritus from the engineering faculty at OSU. He came to this project by a random event: joining it after being a patient of Dr. Martin's, wherein he almost died after having multiple operations for diverticulitis. Dr. Thurston was quiet, unassuming, always inquisitive, smiled a lot, especially when he thought he was on to some significant fact. He treated us surgeons as intellectual equivalents to him, which we all knew was not the case. In my recollections, I recount the hours with Dr. Thurston as golden, be it early in our discussions of radionuclides in autoradiography, or later with a different format, at Biocrystal, another research company, engaged in exploring the expanding possibilities of nano-crystals.

George Hinkle was a young enterprising faculty chemist person, always pleasant, committed to the task of joining radionuclides to glycoprotein molecules, like monoclonal antibodies. He was always helpful and understanding when I fumbled with simple things, for instance working a pipette delivering minute quantities of solution. He published several important papers on the value of various methods to attach the radionuclide 125I to antibodies, and here we make the obvious comment that the clinical aspect of the project always started with this safe chemical process for patient injection.

The patient benefit of the project also never started before Kathy Majzisik and her nurse assistants began getting signed permissions from various authorities, the University, ethics committees, or patients. Kathy was petite, lovely, and wise about every aspect of the project, research, and clinical application in surgery, traveled to demonstrate intricacies of the technique. How Dr. Martin ever found her, I'll never know!

The conferences and meetings, often attracted smart people like Dr. Dave Houchens, my idea of a real, PhD researcher, with experience at NIH, where he worked with Dr. Schlom on the very inception of the monoclonal antibody, thought at first to be the magic bullet for cancer therapy. Dave was employed by Neoprobe Company. He set-up all the pre-clinical experiments, type and doses of antibodies, radionuclides, number of mice required, times of injection, and harvesting. He documented everything, made sure experiments were correct down to the last milligram and minute.

We uncovered untold new features of our tagged antibody entering the planted tumors and entering normal structures as well. Measurements on tumors and normal mouse organs were carefully made with complex Geiger counters so we knew the exact percent of injected radionuclide ending in the tumors as well as normal structures.

We had two different colon tumor lines that were planted in nude mice, one slow growing and the other rapid or so called poorly differentiated. Various Mab's were employed, named, B723, cc49, 17-1A, A5B7, sounds complex but we got to know them all, their characteristics, and the specific antigens that they combined with, in tumors.

However, the detection of the antibody-radionuclide on a microscopic level depended on a known technology called autoradiography, a technique popularized by a book authored by Andrew Rogers, an Australian scientist. How I got into this "cook book" facet of the research is beyond me now, but it served to correlate the Gamma Probe findings and all the results of tissue fragment measurements in Geiger type counters.

The technical details of the craft were complex, but they fit into an association with my time in Country Surgery. Slides prepared in our lab at University, stained routinely or sometimes reacted with immunohistochemistry, I would take to Memorial for further processing with radiographic emulsion. This emulsion, was a white, gelatin laced, milky solution, containing silver bromide crystals, about three hundred dollars ($300.00) per ounce, had to be kept away from light and not bounced around. The slides had to be dipped, always in a completely dark room and put away in light-tight boxes for two weeks or so. The next steps were development with a special solution, then photographic fixation with hypo, all done in the dark with a red safe light. The final product would give tiny dots, microscopic grains, on the slide, showing the exact position of our radionuclide, 125I, with respect to other structures in the tumor or normal tissue. In other words, the emanations from 125I sequestered in the tumor, recorded also by our sensitive probe, changed the silver bromide crystals to metallic silver grains that became visible with the light microscope. You can bet that everyone all over the world jumped on this technology, especially since it was a time when the "magic bullet", the monoclonal antibody, was thought to be the ultimate answer to cancer therapy. This innovation took its moderate place in therapy, but also ultimately for more good, sponsored thousands of other dependent related discoveries.

On the other hand, a research incident occurred at Memorial, which acquired a laughable, humorous twist only in long term retrospect. As things frequently are fraught with emotion during the happening, sometimes, they become amusingly funny as time passes, and one looks back, even adding a few features to tell a good story: Now there was a time when I was "burning the candle at both ends", doing country surgery and autoradiography on tumor sections from OSU at our hospital. A dark room was essential for the latter, and it was my practice to use a room at the end of long basement hall, the morgue. I had selected this seldom used, out of the way, room as the place for me to duct-tape tiny spaces about the entry door preventing light leaks, absolutely essential for processing the research slides. My method was to frequently enter this sanctuary and begin dipping slides in expensive radiographic emulsion, and this was often after a late emergency operation, this one, at about 2:00 A.M.

Somehow, a cleaning lady, working at night, became alarmed by hearing scurrying about in the morgue. She called security; a new man was on duty. They came down, banged on the door and I said from inside: "Go away and don't open this door". Of course I had it locked. He called the local police, they came and of course thinking there was something strange like suicide or murder going on at 3:00 A.M., they demanded opening the door and I repeated the request with emotion but you know, they broke down the door, ruining my experiment, destroying three hundred dollars ($300.00) worth of emulsion and irreplaceable slides of human tumors! I knew the officers from my duty in the emergency room. They were great guys. They said: "Sorry Doc, we'll get the door fixed tomorrow".

Edinburgh

One of our presentations was at Edinburgh in Scotland. We had comparative information about various monoclonal antibodies in colon tumors. One of these, A5B7, was a product of research in London, UK, and we presented our work at a conference at Edinburgh University. It was a combined meeting of the American College of Surgery and The Surgery Society of Scotland. I knew there were few country surgeons given the opportunity to walk the halls of the oldest University in the world and present a paper there – I was nervous; but the finest Scotch whiskey helped.

We made great strides with our autoradiographic techniques – human tumors picked up our conjugates, the same as mouse tumors, often in necrotic areas, indicating that the antibody combined with tumor antigen when its blood level was highest, a few days after injection into the patients. However, as frequently happens in science, confounding results appear: Many lymph nodes draining tumors were probe positive, but pathology could not show cancer cells there. We had "knock-down, dragged-out" debates over this dilemma, enter a Dr. Emilio Barbara, a renowned Spanish scientist, who cultured "what he thought" were cancer cells from the germinal centers of these nodes, but we were showing different reasons for the positive probe counts: The germinal centers of these positive nodes were all showing massive grains over our antibodies, B72,3 or cc49, probably combining with tumor antigen concentrated in these structures. This was not just a hypothetical consideration, but we were actually showing the antigen, a glycoprotein, then called Tag 72, by immunohistochemistry, beneath and complexed with our Mab's as a prominent feature.

There followed a signal paper by Dr. Martin and Dr. Barbera, titled "Resetting the Immune System in Colon Cancer", in which they pointed to a definite survival advantage in patients with all possible probe positive elements removed at surgery. The name given to the overall effort was RIGS, (radio-immuno-guided) surgery, and the object of each operation for colon cancer was to remove all the RIGS, probe positive tumor. The concept was never approved for general use by the FDA, despite good reports entered by several other University centers that used the innovation.

We all struggled with the notion that colon cancer patients showed improved survival after our operations, yet no cancer could be found in many of the structures removed. This dilemma was expressed in the publication by Drs. Martin and Barbera about "Resetting the Immune System." There began in their minds the perception that our own B cell immune system might enhance malignancy, and this persuasion was probably the main reason why they became interested in forming a private research company called Biocrystal. It was located away from the University, but still maintained a connection. One day, Dr. Martin mentioned to me that his research efforts were moving to this new location and that I would be impressed with a fellow out there, a Dr. Barbera, schooled in liver pathophysiology, which we were studying at the time.

Biocrystal, A Private Research Company:

I braved the traffic on and off the freeway one morning and found the Biocrystal building. You can't believe how awe-struck I was at the set-up there and Dr. Barbera gave me the "red carpet" treatment, showing me around and indicating that I could come there to work. It seemed that Dr. Martin had given me a first class introduction, probably telling him of my surgical experience or perhaps of my potential for offering financial support, the farthest thing from my mind. Dr. Barbera treated me as an equal from the outset, called me "Doctor", and I reciprocated with him throughout our association.

The place at Biocrystal, at first, reminded me of scenes from a "James Bond" movie. A business-like reception area with good looking secretaries, small cubicle office spaces lining long hallways, a huge central floor area sectioned off into work spaces with people running machines, welders, workers on small batteries and computer chips, everyone busy. This was the research engineering part of the enterprise. Stairs ran up from this floor to a large surrounding balcony that contained more offices, actually where the main folks hung out, also more labs up there, one containing all the flammable chemicals.

The compartments for biology were fabulous, several big labs, all smartly placed, one with microscopes, untold equipment for cell studies, chemistry, cabinets full of glass containers for measurements. Another on the lower level contained a cryostat, liquid nitrogen container, a new microtome for preparing tissue sections, a flow cytometer unit in a separate side room. Right off this lower lab, through two sets of doors into the mouse room, fancy cages, temperature and light controlled, with alarm mechanisms plus large autoclaves for sterilizing cages and trays. All these labs had double doors, masks and gowns necessary for entry into the chemistry and cell handling area. The labs for dealing with a nanocrystal were in the upper level, controlled by one girl specializing in crystal chemistry. Several other female, technical people that knew everything and ordered everything, once again these girls taught me all about mouse operations, complex mixing of antibodies, plus who was whom about the personnel. A complete work force of folks, just in the biology section, to name a few, Dr. Barbera, in charge of biology research, Dr. Thurston, Dr. Martin came intermittently, three graduate students, and not to forget a sharp manager, Jeff Bergan, plus, the main mogul Dr. John Howard, a former engineering student of Dr. Thurston, as CEO, investment producer, in charge of the whole works, engineering as well as biology.

They gave me a small cubicle with a microscope on a circular desk, and at first I went there two days a week because I was still operating at Memorial, but soon to retire. What a chance positive series of events for me – to move from an active surgical practice into an all-encompassing research activity. It seemed to me that the projects at Biocrystal were unlimited: the main theme, carried over from work at University, was that the B cell immune system, enhanced cancer. Specific antibody, combining with tumor cell antigen produced complexes, bringing macrophages and neutrophils, enhancing angiogenesis. Our group was one of the first to accent the role of macrophages in providing the stimulus for blood vessel production (through vascular-endothelial growth factor) in tumors and in adjacent microenvironment – all positive for cancer development and progression.

Our thinking, of course, was that this cascade was interrupted in colon cancer when RIGS removed main tumor masses along with the B cell active probe positive lymph nodes, thus accounting for increased survival in many patients. A further hypothetical plus, we could never prove, was the destructive action of 125I on microscopic events necessary for secondary B cell production of antibody, on dendritic processes in geminal centers of probe positive lymph nodes.

We had hundreds of unique experiments with mice and different types of cancer cells, lung, breast, melanoma, all studies related to the theory. One excellent model for producing liver metastasis was splenic injection of tumor cells. Locally recurrent tumor was also studied by excising subcutaneous growths after a certain time lapse, altering mouse strains, blocking B cell activity with antibodies, all aimed at the same possible end point. We published numerous papers in prestigious journals. My role was primarily in Pathology and immunohistochemistry.

When we had an outstanding triumph, like publishing a significant paper, or an entry accepted at an important meeting, out came the champagne to celebrate. One such triumph with our nanocrystals was when Dr. Barbera and I teamed to insert a small canula in the portal vein of a mouse, then injected a solution of wheat germ agglutinin coupled with our fluorescent nanocrystals, to show the complex fixed in central veins of liver lobules. We photographed this phenomenon and the enlarged photo hung in the main hall for months, a beautiful bright yellow outline of the central vein's lining endothelium. It was a symbol for the chemist's efforts to attach nanocrystals to other molecules, including glycoproteins. The photo was taken by the fluorescent microscope, worth about $100,000 dollars, with all its computer components, loaned to us on a deal through Zeiss manufacturing, stipulating the arrangement that they would use the photos we took for display at their advertising exhibits.

Money seemed to be no object at the institution: A girl named Barbara was the important person in charge of supply, and when one needed an antibody, chemical or instrument, one just put in a requisition. I never knew where finances came from, nor did I have any inkling into the workings of how capital was raised for an independent research company. Evidently, there were people out there ready to invest in a company with the hope some invention or concept would materialize and increase their net worth. John Howard called me in one day and insisted I consider pay for my work at the company: My relationship at the University had always been volunteer, and I assumed the same situation would apply at Biocrystal. But John demanded that I take $500.00 per month, and I agreed to a plan he suggested, apply the money into Biocrystal Company stock.

You can guess that I was into this research with "full go", now retired from surgery at Memorial, up every morning at 4:00 or 5:00 a.m., drive to the lab to cut tissue or start an antibody experiment early so that I could finish by 5:00 P.M. Weekly and sometimes daily meetings with the group, setting deadlines, discussions with young people, learning from then about computers and oncoming molecular genetics. We gave a few seminars at Otterbein College for the pre-med and science students about the practical aspects of immunology. These were fun!

Dr. Barbera and company queried the idea of getting a million dollar grant to study the cancer patients at Memorial Hospital of Union County, and I got the immediate enthusiastic permission of the then hospital administrator. Dr. Martin was the faculty member that connected the research with a clinical component at the University through the James Cancer Center. There actually was one clinical project of B cell depression, in a few patients with advanced colon cancer, suggesting at least stabilization of their disease.

So, here was a "Camelot" situation, everyone working and happy, an ideal set up, basic research with a clinical connection, all sorts of possibilities for human good, medical, financial, not to mention the basic developments with a new device for cell culture and the nanocrystal projects.

The Beginning Of Camelot's Demise:

But life can be a "screw-up", and chance perturbations can alter personalities like you can't imagine! I'm on the outside looking in, so I'll never know the entire details of the entanglements, nor do I want to – but the initial event occurred one morning when I came in and Julie, the PhD candidate, with her cubicle right across from mine, told me "We are no longer associated with the University." "Why?", I asked. "Because", she said, "they had a big argument over patent rights, Dr. Barbera called Dr. Martin "a meager technician in the company" and Dr. Martin responded with some other superlative!

From that day onward things were never the same. Money became a problem, several of the girls, profoundly knowledgeable, including the chemist that worked with nanocrystals, were let go! A Chinese PhD, chemist, schooled in recombinant molecular genetic techniques, recently hired, was also removed. Someone hired an investigator with a long Arab name. The young people had difficulty working with him, because "he did not consider us equal individuals" they said.

James W. Sampsel

Further Nails In The Coffin:

About a month later, an event came about, I could hardly believe: The company lawyers brought a law suit against Dr. Martin for utilizing some alleged privileged information acquired at Biocrystal, sharing it with other physicians in a study at the University. It got complicated when a counter suit was filed, but all was overshadowed by another episode that sealed the doom of Biocrystal. Rumor had it that John and Dr. Barbera also had a confrontation, after which Dr. Barbera had to leave the premises, collect his belongings, and never return. I am sure uncontrolled emotions characterized this whole series of incidents. One side claimed Dr. B's behavior unjustified, irrational, even threatening, but there was no confirmation of this, and I noticed Dr. B. eventually just faded away. Perhaps John and company simply thought he was a poor Director of Research? But it was the "beginning of the end" for Biocrystal. In my humble opinion, as an outside observer, knowing nothing of the financial arrangements, only the science, Dr. B. was the guiding influence for every project. There were other folks with specific interests, but no one with his insight into multiple disciplines, immunology, pathology, oncology, basic biology, cell culture, crystal chemistry, even the new molecular genetics. He could speak and write in four languages. I have this "back of my mind" idea about people trying to take advantage of Dr. B. in legal matters because of his Spanish origin and perhaps a misguided opinion regarding his knowledge of the English language.

The conflict for Dr. Barbera with Biocrystal and John, the former CEO, generated a lawyer's dream, with intellectual property rights, patent ownerships, financial appropriation, all a far cry from lecturing students and thinking science. The legal shenanigans went on for several years. I was prepared to testify, but never was called: hopefully, Dr. B. attained a reasonable settlement. Even with time altering the mental image, for me, it is still difficult to understand how so many learned individuals can have a complete change in mind-set about each other: in some cases, tolerance to condemnation, but in others, initial adulation for years, changing to objection and accusation. As an example of the latter, several people about the University told me they <u>thought</u> Dr. B. copied other people's work and that he knowingly altered data, all "baloney" in my mind. Nearly everyone copies some other's work; that is why we have bibliographies. There can often be differences of opinion about certain results, but falsifying data: never!

So, I sided with Dr. B., and the last years of my research efforts were out of his home laboratory, where we worked on several considerations: one was an arrangement he somehow achieved with the Professor of Immunology at Otterbein College to help in science teaching there. For months, we went two days a week, lectured, assisted in basic tasks, like creating monoclonal antibodies, isolating RNA and DNA in tumor cells, cell culture techniques – all philanthropic, for the joy of working with the students, and a possible different approach to our theme: B cell activity enhancing cancer. We had great fun there, ending each day with student sessions, in a local hang-out, eating rolls and drinking coffee.

Our efforts at Otterbein College ended rather abruptly, before many students actually finished their projects. Possibly, the Professor worried about being out-done by Dr. B., or somewhat likely a far-out warning from Biocrystal. John Howard was a member of the college associated church and a heavy contributor, so a natural move was to inform the Professor that Dr. B. was a bad fellow and to curtail his activities within the department.

We returned to the home lab and Dr. B concentrated on developing his new cell culture device. It was a thin, closed system, had to have cells and media injected via a syringe, but there were many advantages over the customary flask, the latter used since the science began.

It was during these days at the home lab where I learned about Dr. Barbera's life and science career: packed with vital steps, medical school in Germany, PhD thesis on platelet development from mega karyocytes, dean of a medical school in Spain for years, worked with Nobel prize people in England, brilliant writer and researcher. It was in this environment that I was privileged to end my official research with a study on colon cancer. We wrote several chapters in books on cancer, drawing on our past experiences at Biocrystal and had published several papers on the dynamics of oxygen in cultured cells.

Some of the philosophical gems that we discussed during these sessions: When reviewing work, the premise: "The only thing I know for sure is that there's nothing I know for sure".

He asked me: "If there's a heaven, do I get to go there and look into a microscope for eternity?"

When I showed him photographs of eosinophils being present about and over dead colon cancer cells he would say: "If you walked into a room and saw a dead man on the floor, another standing over him with a smoking gun, you would have to assume who did the murder."

If you stumble on an important discovery, report it and no one takes it up, either they are stupid or you may be wrong!

All of these gems probably sound better in Spanish.

We actually accomplished a lot more there, but this finishes my chapter on research, but for me it will never really be finished. I have this outmoded interest in the human condition, be it on a simple microscopic level or associated with my own complex brain function. There is always the chance that I could stumble on some random event that would be important out there to relieve pain or quiet anxiety. World's research in vogue now centers about molecular genetics, sequencing genes, protein production, converting body cells into pluri-potent stem types even direct change in formation without the intermediate stem phase, lots of things to keep young folks busy, in the future, for pleasant journeys.

Finis:

My wife had tears in her eyes as we watched the records and furniture being carted out of our office, which we occupied for some thirty years. The records of patients, thousands of them, were on their way to storage for two years before being destroyed. Each record in its manila folder represented part of a life story for an individual. Picking out a few, reading them, seeing the name, I visualized the person, and I was surprised at the number of visits along with the record of each, down to the last detail.

Closing the office was a sad event for us, and leaving my position at the hospital was the same. But ever declining physical capabilities, the effort necessary to stand over cases for hours, the mental anguish, all became realities. Add to this my reluctance to embark on training for new techniques like fiberoptic surgery and the increasing hazards of incidents being construed as malpractice. Meanwhile, we also acquired well-trained individuals to continue the surgical specialties, with no legal entanglements. All these features helped to bring our time in county surgery to a close.

There can be a certain inner satisfaction with the concept that: "About everything must come to an end". This is true in my mind, except with time and perhaps the universe. Your time, my time, products of our brain function, Memorial Hospital time as well, all have a beginning and an end. But time itself, always there, how could it have had a beginning? or an end? At least we can think of something out there for sure, time, nebulous and fleeting, with no beginning and no end! A good way to ponder the finis!

The author draws on his experiences in training and the military, leading into forty-five productive years of general surgery at a county hospital. Impressions of time on the clinical faculty of a major university, with research efforts, are also included. The good and occasionally the bad, as part of every life, accented.

CPSIA information can be obtained at www.ICGtesting.com
Printed in the USA
244678LV00002B/10/P